The Zeppelin air-raids on Hull and East Yorkshire

Arthur G Credland

East Yorkshire Local History Society
2023

EYLHS Series No.66

Series editor Arthur G Credland

ISBN 10   0-900349-66-2 / ISBN 13   978-0-900349-66-9

EAN 9780900349669

Printed by Kall Kwik, Hull

Leslie W.G. Credland 1937-2022

This publication is dedicated to the memory of my late brother. He was not a 'joiner' but took a great interest in the EYLHS and its publications though never becoming a member. His bequest to the Society will enable us to produce more frequent special publications and it seemed appropriate for me to offer this topic, the Zeppelin raids, given his keen interest in aeronautics, and particularly its local manifestations.

The Zeppelin air-raids on Hull and East Yorkshire

Arthur G. Credland

The present writer has previously published a detailed account of the Zeppelin airship raids on Hull and of the public reaction, against the backdrop of the attacks across the country as a whole.[1] The material that follows is from a variety of sources which reveal the nature of Zeppelin attacks across East Yorkshire as well as the effects of the eight raids on Hull. Though Goole has only recently been included in East Yorkshire it is appropriate to include a description of the devastation caused by bombing on a densely populated area near the docks which resulted in 16 deaths.[2] Goole was a significant target, though in this instance an accidental one, being the key to the canal system connecting the industry and commerce of the West Riding with the Ouse and the Humber.

Hull had a number of steam whistles installed across the city, usually described in the press and official sources as 'buzzers',[3] but the eyewitness accounts quoted below refer to them as 'hooters'.[4] Originally these were intended as a signal for all lights to be turned off so as to maintain a black out[5] until the 'dismiss' (all clear) was sounded, as well as to call out the Specials, and signal the ambulance crews to be in readiness. Their sounds became however a signal for hundreds, indeed thousands, of people to leave their homes for the safety of the open spaces of the nearest park, or to walk out into the countryside. This phenomenon, which became known as 'trekking', was repeated in the 1939-45 war.

The 'buzzer' originally installed at the Blundell and Spence factory, at the corner of Beverley road,[6] is preserved in the Hull Museum to which it was given at the end of the 1914-18 war. Each, identifiable to the hearer by its unique pitch and tone, was given a name, in this case 'Lizzie.' It was removed from the museum for use in the Second World War and subsequently returned there, with a brief summary of its history engraved on the surface of the brass casing (figs. 1a, b).[7]

1a, b. Steam whistle; warning buzzer installed at Blundell and Spence, Beverley road, Hull (Hull Museums).

An account of the Zeppelin raids in Yorkshire and north east appeared in the *Yorkshire Post* after the end of the Great War when the reporting restrictions in force during hostilities had finally been lifted. Norfolk had received the first bombs dropped by Zeppelins to land on English soil, 19 January 1915, killing four people and injuring 16. The north of England was attacked, 14-15 April, 1915, when Zeppelin L9, commanded by Kapitanleutnant Mathy approached the Northumberland coast about 1 am, flying over Blyth, Bedlington, Morpeth, Wallsend and Hebburn and then passed out to sea two miles south of South Shields. Bombs were dropped seemingly at random, caused little damage, and no lives were lost (fig. 2).

ZEPPELIN RAID MEMORIAL.

Press Bureau. OFFICIAL MESSAGE.
"**Zeppelins visited the Eastern Counties** on Tuesday night (17th August, 1915), dropped bombs, resulting in **10 killed and 36 injured.** Some houses and other buildings, including a church, were damaged."

The Midnight Assassin

2. Postcard memorialising Zeppelin raid in the North East, 1915 (Hull History Centre).

Large areas of the country, embracing vital naval and military sites became 'prohibited areas' accessible to citizens with proper identification but completely forbidden to aliens and suspect persons. These included the major ports, the east coast, much of the south coast and a greater part of Scotland. Permits were issued giving the recipient access to restricted areas (fig.3) and the problems of negotiating one's way into and out of these areas without this documentation is featured in the Richard Hannay story, *Mr. Standfast.*[8]

The account in the *Yorkshire Post* gives a description of the mixed results of raids into East Yorkshire:

> Seven weeks later just after midnight, Friday 4 June 1915, a Zeppelin appeared over the Yorkshire coast, first spotted from Bridlington in the early hours of Saturday morning. Bombs were dropped on Driffield in an orchard near the Beckside, tearing up and splitting the fruit trees in all directions, and slicing the vegetable crops as if they had been cut with a scythe. All the cottages within a hundred yards were so shaken that there was hardly one with an unbroken window. Beyond a few cuts and bruises sustained by one or two women, there was no call for the services of the medical men who were promptly on the spot. Very few people witnessed the subsequent flight of

the airship over the wolds. Those who did were of the opinion that the pilot had lost his way. He appeared to go westward in the direction of Sledmere, and then take a course south of Driffield, then making eastward for Bridlington Bay. [9]

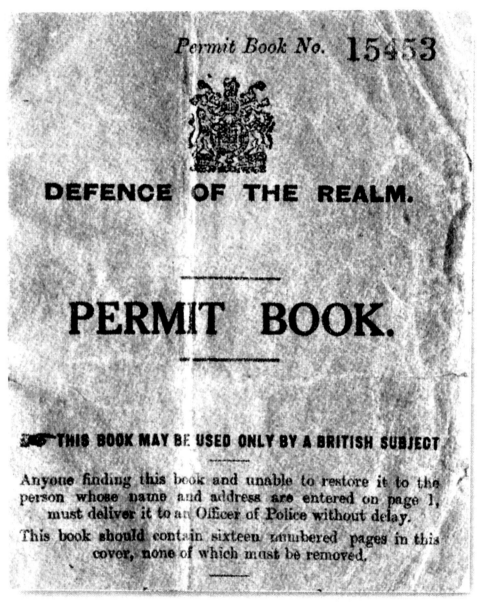

Permit Book No. 15453

DEFENCE OF THE REALM.

PERMIT BOOK.

THIS BOOK MAY BE USED ONLY BY A BRITISH SUBJECT

Anyone finding this book and unable to restore it to the person whose name and address are entered on page 1, must deliver it to an Officer of Police without delay. This book should contain sixteen numbered pages in this cover, none of which must be removed.

3. Permit for access to restricted areas (Internet).

****

The Driffield Times 28 December 1918
The Zeppelin Outrages

Now that the ban has been removed respecting the publication of news of raids made by the Zepps, it may be of interest to recall the fact that Driffield was the first Yorkshire town to have bombs dropped by these murderous machines. The event was made on Friday, June 4th, 1915, when the machine was seen somewhere in the neighbourhood of the parish church, about 11 p.m. It was ascertained that it had entered by way of Bridlington, and after reaching Driffield, seemed to be in doubt as to its whereabouts[10]. It then cruised round by Langtoft and Sledmere, eventually passing over Driffield on its way home, about 1 a.m. on the Saturday morning. Two bombs were dropped, which caused great explosions, startling many of the inhabitants of the town and district from

4a. Bomb crater at rear of Springfield House, Eastgate South, Driffield; note the loss of tiles from the roof of the house (Treasure House, Beverley).

4b. Bomb crater off Meadow Lane, Driffield (Treasure House, Beverley).

their slumbers. The first bomb was dropped in the garden behind Springfield House, in Eastgate South, doing considerable damage to the root crops and surrounding trees. The houses in the neighbourhood were also much shaken, and some hundreds of squares of glass were broken, while pieces of shrapnel were picked up at great distances from the scene of the explosion, and many people received cuts from broken glass. There was only an interval of a few minutes between the explosions, the second bomb falling in a field in Meadow Lane, belonging to Mr. Walmsley, opposite the first gate house, where it made a large cavity, very much resembling a pond, but no other damage was done.

Rumours spread, which were greatly exaggerated, and the town was visited by thousands of people on the Saturday and Sunday, many coming from Hull, who expressed their astonishment at so slight a damage.

Many people had the impression that this visit was one of searching out for a good landing,[11] and this would appear to be correct, for on the following Sunday night another Zeppelin came over Bridlington and Driffield and found its way to Hull, doing a great deal of damage.

This brought lighting restrictions more strongly into force, and Special Constables were enrolled to do duty on 'Air raid warning' nights, and although we have had many warnings, and Zeppelins passing over the town, which caused the inhabitants much worry and anxiety, we have been very fortunate that no further bombs were dropped in Driffield, after seeing what other towns have experienced (figs.4a,b).

****

Magazine of Bridlington High School Christmas 1915[12]
A Zeppelin scare

We had a very thrilling time one night last term. We were all sleeping peacefully the sleep of the just, and the hard-worked, when suddenly an insistent but reassuring voice awakened us: 'Come along, girls, down to the cellars quickly. No! its quite all right, you needn't be afraid.' We all tumbled out of bed and scrambled wildly for dressing gowns, slippers and clothing of all description. Finally we got everything gathered together and started off helter-skelter down the back stairs, some half asleep, some laughing, some very quakey, and others very cool, so much so that one remarkable person had the presence of mind to take her knitting. Most of us weren't in this happy state, and distinguished ourselves by strewing the stairs and passages with our things, treading on people's toes and making a general nuisance of ourselves. At last, after what seemed to us about an hour on the way, we got to the cellars and settled down quite happily for the night. It was a great business to find room for us all, but in the end most of us found places and huddled up on the floor in rugs and blankets. In one corner was a big bath, into which nearly everyone threw her bundle of clothes, and two sleepy persons climbed into it and tried to continue their peaceful sleep. They had about the most comfortable place of anyone. After a time everybody got rather bored, so one of the cool and collected persons brought and read aloud to the assembled company a most melodramatic novel: a rumour of this reached the kitchen, where the mistresses had taken up their abode and one or two of them went to listen to the inspiring words of the infant prodigy. After about an hour light refreshments, in the shape of tea and biscuits were handed round to everyone's great delight. We were awfully disgusted because we were not allowed to go outside to see if we could catch a glimpse of the fateful Zeppelin, or even to hear the guns. It really was rather disappointing to have had all this trouble and then not to hear anything about it. About one o'clock the police rang through that all was safe, so we trotted back to bed, and in our dormitory had nearly all from the top floor on mattresses between our beds, making a total of sixteen instead of eight. Thus ended our first real experience of Zeppelin scares, and, on the whole, it was really quite well enjoyed by all.

E. Johnson, V.

The entries in bold type which follow are from the diaries of Margaret Elizabeth Strickland-Constable (1873-1961)[13], who was 'commandant' of the Brooklands Officers Hospital, 171/173 Cottingham road, and the V.A.D. hospital, Hornsea.[14] She seems totally unfased by medical emergencies and air raids alike:

1915

June 5th **The postman brought the news that there had been Zeppelins at Driffield and that ambulances had been going from Hull all night. George sent up to ask if he might go over & see his parents were safe, at 11 a.m. he came back & reported that no one was injured but that 3 bombs had been dropped, one in a field near to the station, and in a villa garden which had damaged some apple-trees & another in the outskirts.**

Andrew Bethell[15] came to lunch with his wounded shoulder - Mellors announced him as 'Master Adrian' & he said, 'How are you, Mr. Mellors?' from force of habit. A. said he had been to a dance in London, but had not danced, as he thought it such a mistake to have a dance at all. He also said he thought 'war-weddings' a 'great folly'. He said Hilary[16] was the prettiest little girl he had ever seen.[17]

At the hospital we were warned to be ready to proceed at once to the hospital, in uniform & bearing the Geneva brassard [red cross arm band] **in case of an air-raid. I offered to sleep at the hospital if they wished it. We placed a bucket of water on the landings, & inspected the cellars where there are candles, biscuits, & water in readiness.**

One of the patients had tried to cut his throat and help was needed from medical staff in Hull to deal with the persistent bleeding of the carotid artery:

He wired to Hull for Dr. Harrison who said there was an air-raid scare, all the lights turned out, & that he could not drive out till daylight, so we continued to hold the artery [ie.using finger compression] **all night, with the help of Mrs. Brodrick, who came up about 11. At 4.30 Dr. Harrison came, the boy was given chloroform, & Dr. H. tied the arteries in 3 or 4 places & stitched him up again. I wore the india-rubber gloves & swabbed for him, & threaded the needles & held the arteries and released the forceps when required.**

****

A lucid description of the path of the Zeppelin from the coast towards Hull, for the city's first attack is given in the *Yorkshire Post*[18]:

The airship appears to have passed over Bridlington Bay, following the railway line from Hornsea to Hull, and after attacking the city, returned by way of the Humber, taking a course between Immingham and Grimsby to the sea. The first bombs were dropped near Sculcoates Station on the Holderness Road. They fell upon some working-class tenement houses in Waller Street, the backs of which run parallel to the station, and smashed them to pieces, killing several persons and injuring many more. One terrace in this street containing fourteen houses was almost completely demolished.(fig.5)

From Southcoates the airship sailed towards Dansom Lane, where an incendiary bomb was thrown upon Messrs. Hewitt and Cos. timber yard, which was soon in a blaze, and several adjoining houses were partially demolished. The airship then went in the direction of Rank's great flour mills in Clarence street, and a bomb was thrown upon a row of cottages in East Street, where three persons were buried in the debris. A boy named Edward Jordan was literally blown to pieces.

From this point the raider steered over Church street near Drypool Green, and laid a number of houses in ruins. A corner house abutting upon Church Street and St. Paul's Avenue had both walls of both storeys completely torn out, leaving one of the bedroom floors sloping at a dangerous angle. Several substantial front houses, each containing six to eight rooms, were completely destroyed, but, although there were injuries to residents, not a single life was lost here.

From Church Street the airship crossed the River Hull, sailed in the vicinity of the General Post Office, and dropped a bomb into the Queen's Dock beside the new Guildhall. In this part of the town excited crowds were shouting and scurrying for shelter as explosion followed explosion. When the commotion was at its height incendiary bombs were dropped upon the great drapery establishment of Messrs. Edwin Davies[sic] and Co., in the Market Place, which instantly burst into flames, and within a few minutes explosive missiles were wrecking warehouses and offices in the neighbouring High Street.

Holy Trinity Church, adjoining [Edwin Davis] had a marvellous escape. Only a few yards separated the building from the south side of the historic church-in fact the flames were scorching its venerable walls and cracking its windows- while on the

5. Walter's Terrace, Waller street; taken 7 June 1915, after the first Zeppelin raid on Hull, photographed by Charles Turner (Hull Museums).

north side a shell had been dropped on the roof of the Corn Exchange Hotel, but failed to explode, and was handed over to the military authorities.

The fire at the drapery establishment defied all efforts to subdue it. It lit up the entire area of Central Hull and the conflagration was at its height before the Zeppelin left the city. Despite the efforts of the special constables to close the streets, thousands of people from all directions flocked to the scene, where also the fire brigade promptly appeared, with companies of soldiers to help the firemen. There was no use in pouring water upon the burning shops. They were a red-hot mass, and every wall and pillar was gradually falling, bringing storey after storey to the ground. Happily in a couple of hours, all danger of the fire spreading was removed, and the old church was safe. Fortunately there were no employees on the drapery shop premises, otherwise the result would have been appalling. Messrs. Davies' loss was afterwards estimated at £100,000 (figs.6a,b,c).

6a, b. Destruction of Edwin Davis, drapers; the smouldering ruins adjacent to Holy Trinity church, 7 June 1915, after the first raid.

In the Old Town and West Hull

In the Old Town area enormous damage was done to small house property between the Market Place and the High Street. One bomb bored a hole fully 20 feet deep in diameter in front of the premises of T.W. Palmer and Co.[19] and Messrs. John Good and Sons,[20] completely blocking the street. Many old buildings were shaken to their foundations and doomed to destruction; in fact nearly all the houses in Grimsby Lane presented a shattered front of broken glass. Further south, off Queen Street, which is a continuation of Market Place to the Pier, there was a loss of life as well as wreckage of old property. Three boys named Mullins, at 39 Blanket Row, were badly burned in a fire caused by an incendiary bomb.

From the old town the Zeppelin crossed the Queen's Dock near the Wilberforce monument, over the electric power station of the City Tramways undertaking, and bombs were dropped in Albert Terrace, Pease Street, Porter Street and Walker Street. The bomb in Albert Terrace did not completely explode, and a soldier living near poured water over it and handed it to the police. Three bombs fell in Porter Street. The house, 2 Sarah Ann's Place was set in a blaze, Mrs Emma Pickering, a widow, 68 years of age, was burnt to death. At the house, 22, Edwin's Place, Mrs Georgiana Cunningham, 27 years of age, was killed in her bed, a bomb passing through her bedroom and wrecking the house next door. Her child who lay beside her was uninjured; but her husband did not escape. He was terribly crushed, and taken to the Infirmary. At no.21, a painter, named William Watson, aged 67, and his wife, Annie Watson, aged 58, were instantly killed, and so badly mutilated that identification was extremely difficult. The house was practically blown up.

The Porter street district furnished a striking example of the difference between the effect of high explosive bombs and that of incendiary bombs. In Edwin's Place a bomb of the former type dropped on a cottage. The little house, as well as those on either side of it, was completely destroyed. All the houses in the court, perhaps 20 in all, were very much damaged and rendered uninhabitable, and a number of persons were injured. Roofs were stripped off, windows and doors blown in, and furniture and crockery smashed (fig 7a,b).

6c. A view northwards from equestrian monument of King William III, towards the ruined store.

Two well-known streets in West Hull, South Parade and Campbell Street -suffered badly at the hands of the raider, and several persons were killed. In Campbell Street a block of front houses, with a terrace running off the street, all lying between St. Thomas's Church and Messrs Holmes Tannery, were tumbled into ruins(fig.8a,b,c). The roof and north side of the church were dismantled and scores of windows in the tannery and adjacent houses were broken. The house, 2 St. Thomas's Terrace, was terribly smashed from roof to floor. The occupants, William Walker, aged 62, a tanner's labourer, with his two daughters, Alice Priscilla, aged 30, and Millicent, aged 17, were killed outright, and his wife was conveyed to the Naval Hospital seriously injured. In South Parade an incendiary bomb struck the house occupied by Mr. Maurice Richardson, setting it on fire, and his son Maurice age 11, and daughter Violet, aged 9, perished in the flames. The Zeppelin then steered a course along the Anlaby Road, dropping several bombs in Coltman Street and Constable Street, where little damage was done. A shell [sic]was dropped in a field opposite the Anlaby Garden Village Estate [ie. Anlaby Park], which

7a. Damage to Porter street after the first raid, 6/7 June 1915.

7b. Great Thornton street, home of the Needler family, showing the spartan living conditions. Five boys were sleeping in this room, two in the bed struck by an incendiary which penetrated the ceiling and the floor, landing on bed of Mrs Needler who was seriously burned;7 June 1915.Photograph by Charles Turner (Hull Museums).

lies in the direction of the Springhead Waterworks and followed the Humber towards the east.' [21]

Apparently having exhausted the supply of explosive bombs only incendiaries were dropped on Grimsby :-

One struck a railway siding on the docks, setting fire to two empty goods trucks; and one or two bombs fell into the water of the Royal Dock. Another bomb dropped in Fish Dock Road, striking in its descent, the wall of the Joint Ice Factory. The bomb burnt itself out without doing any damage, although in its fall it missed, by only a few feet, the great ammonia tanks at the works. Another incendiary bomb fell near a

8a. Photograph by Watson, of house in Campbell street; from souvenir booklet, Hull Daily News (Hull Museums).

8b. St. Thomas Terrace, Campbell street, 7 June 1915; a photograph by Charles Turner (Hull Museums).

8c. St.Thomas Terrace, Campbell street,7 June 1915; the church in the background. Photograph by Charles Turner (Hull Museums).

railway crossing, while yet another, striking the roadway in Freeman Street, close to St. Andrew's Church, burnt itself out harmlessly.

After passing over the town, the airship took a south-easterly course, and was not again seen.'[22]

****

Letter written by Rosa Chant to her daughters Jesse and Gladys who were staying in Hornsea, the morning after the first Zeppelin raid on Hull[23] :

29 The Woodlands
Beverley

Safe home- Safe home in port
Dearest girlies-
Did you have a visitor last night & did it alarm you much?
We heard it - The first time I've heard a Zeppelin They told us it had come to Hornsea
& we just had to leave you in Hands that were better able to take care of You than we
were-Miss Kirk will tell us about You-please –I'm longing to see you both-
Love to Edie
& all
Yours
Mother

****

Contination of Margaret Strickland-Constable's diary :

June 6 '15 Fred[24] told me we ought to sleep on the ground floor because of Zeppelins, & I said it was too much trouble. However, at 10.50 a.m. there came the most horrible buzzing roaring noise just over our heads, & we all said 'Zeppelins' & I went to lock the door of the safe which I had left open. Presently there came another, much nearer & circled round rather undecidedly, so I woke Robert, & picked up Hilary, pink dressing gown, white monkey,& all,& put them to bed in the drawing room. There Gertie, Bates [?] & I returned to the upper windows & sat there listening, counting the bombs being dropped on poor old Hull, & the gun-fire in return, & presently we saw an ominous red light in the sky. All was quiet by 12, in fact the owls had never stopped hooting, & the thick white blanket of mist made everything absolutely peaceful all the time. It was a most curious feeling, seeing nothing & hearing this sinister sound overhead, with something of the horrible note in it that there is in a lion's roar. It was dreadful, too to sit listening to the 20 bombs being dropped at regular intervals, and to know that each meant death to many, without the smallest possibility of defence.

News cutting pasted into the diary:
The secretary of the Admiralty yesterday made the following announcement:
A Zeppelin visited the East Coast during last night. Incendiary and explosive bombs, were dropped, causing two fires and resulting in five deaths and forty being injured.

June 8th This is the notice that has appeared in all the papers this morning-a very mild description considering that there were 100 deaths [actually a quarter of that figure], one whole street demolished, & numbers of small houses wrecked. We went to Hull yesterday, June 7th, Edwyn [sic] Davis's big drapery shop was a pile of smoking ashes, with 2 fire-engines still playing on it. We saw another house in Bright street that had been burnt down, visited about 5 houses that were quite pathetic with their squalid interiors all laid open & crumbled to powder. We spoke to a woman with a bandaged head who said quite proudly, 'Everyone on this side of the street is wounded'. Then we had felt we had seen enough that was depressing, & came away. Col. & Mrs. Beresford came to tea to-day-a telegram had come at 9.40 on Sunday to say 'Zeppelin approaching quickly be prepared'. The Zep. came on at Aldborough & flew over Hornsea on to Flamborough Head, then returned south & circled over this house for 10 minutes, & flew off towards Hull. It dropped a bright green light on the shore at Hornsea which they describe as very terrifying. The legend of the big grey motor that guides them is revived[25]-Mrs Beresford says she saw it! Col. B. is much amused by the excitement at the Hydro - 2 maids fainted, & when the engineer was told to turn off the lights he rushed away & never came back. The young officers rushed about asking, 'What can I do to help, sir?', and some of them, who had arrested four supposed spies on their own account rang him up to ask what on earth they were to do with them, as they had turned out to be perfectly respectable people. The bulldog never stirred the whole time.[26]
[The coroner told Mrs. Bates that he had held 26 inquests for the Hull victims[27]]

June 8th Tuesday At 10 p.m. we heard the hooter going in Hull, & we were told that 6 Zeppelins had left Germany, & that one was approaching the Humber.
June 9th Rumours became wilder & wilder, now that no information is published. Newcastle, Tynemouth, Scarbro', Grimsby, King' Cross, & Charing X, are all reported to have been attacked. Fred never took his clothes off all last night – he came over & took me to Driffield to see the bomb-holes there. The Zepp. had made a perfectly clean-cut circular saucer-shaped hole (in a field), 7 yards across & 6 ft. deep in the centre. No debris to be seen anywhere. The hole in a cottage garden

was similar, but the gooseberry-bushes & apple trees around it were blackened & burnt-looking.

June 10th Thursday We got out of the motor & walked down Spyvee St. [in Hull], which we had been told was totally destroyed (As a matter of fact it was quite untouched). While we were gone a crowd of women surrounded the motor declaring that we were spies, & George only pacified them by telling that it was Colonel Constable's car. One of the women said her husband was in the 3d East Yorks., & that she had seen Col. Constable, so then they were satisfied (Observe the logic.) A police-inspector came that way, & we asked him about the damage, and he advised us not to go down side streets, as the people are so excited there is no knowing what they might do. They had told him that some ladies had come in a motor, & might be spies, & that was why he had come that way. Fred told me that Mrs. Turner, wife of Col. Turner of the 3rd Leicesters, was walking on the road from Hedon to Hull, and had found a boot <u>with a foot in it</u> ,at least 3 miles outside Hull.

<u>Rumours</u> This morning include that the 'little grey motor' had been caught at last, near Dalton Holme, & the driver shot; he had a flash-light on his wrist, & wireless apparatus which he worked with his foot. The Zepp. which was brought down at Ghent on Monday was the same one that was here on Saturday night,& the pilot had no legs! Really it was well worth while to give up our private letter-bag, (a war-economy) to hear all these rumours, which are brought by the postman every morning.

This evening we had authentic information that there has been no fresh raid on London-the post-mistress said to Gertie, 'Perhaps I ought not to tell you, but there is a lady staying at the rectory.' Very characteristic of the country.

June 11th
---------------- Someone said that 50,000 people from Hull had spent night after the air-raid in the fields. An attack is expected to-night. I believe.

The motor (or cycle) that everyone declared was guiding the Zeps. to Hull on Sunday turned out to have belonged to Arthur Coulson (our former groom), who was returning to Hull that night & was racing the air-ship all the way in order to warn the town. He is employed at a garage.

June 13 There was an alarm last night, it appears, but we knew nothing of it. 50,000 people from Hull from Hull slept in the fields outside the town for 3 nights after the raid.

Two men (Sir. R. Walker's agent & Will Stenton's nephew) have been mobbed in Hull because they were looking at the ruins.

June 18 Was in a hat shop in Hull & found a stout woman there paying 3/6 to have her best hat done up, which had been injured by a bomb.----------------

June 19th Margot's rumours grow wilder-500 people killed at Newcastle on the 16th, & 3 docks totally destroyed.-------------

June 23 Surgeon General Ferris inspected the hospital, & said it was the best equipped hospital in the 6 counties. He told us we should get no wounded at present, as we are in 'the danger-zone' – no more are to be sent to Hull, as the

wounded in the Naval Hospital [28]**were so much upset by the Zeppelin raid on June 6th, but he told us (to console us) that the work we were doing was quite as useful!**

June 28. 15. **A sea-plane had arrived at Atwick (by train). After the Hull raid Lord Nunburnholme**[29] **is said to have gone to the Admiralty & asked for more efficient protection- is this the entirely effective measures that Mr. Batford has stated to have been taken.**

After the first raid on London 31 May 1915 strict censorship was imposed, both to prevent the enemy discovering the effectiveness or otherwise, of the bombing, and to prevent alarm and panic across the nation. This was an inevitable response because though the pre-war German spy network in Britain had been thoroughly shut down any reports in the newspapers could be picked up abroad and quickly republished in the neutral countries (Holland, the U.S.A. etc). Neutral shipping was still coming into British ports and there were several attempts by the German intelligence service to infiltrate men into Britain masquerading as passengers or crew.

****

HULL: First Zeppelin raid L95 Kapitanleutnant Heinrich Mathy, one of the most daring airship commanders, Sunday and Monday, 6/7 June 1915:

Fatalities[30]
Hull Coroner's Inquests, 8 June
1. 6664[31] **Maurice (William) Richardson** 11, son of Maurice Septimus Richardson, driver Royal Fortress Artillery, 9th Scottish Division, British Expeditionary Force (rullyman before the war), 50 South Parade, Anlaby road died 6 June] *Injuries sustained by the explosion of bombs discharged by a German Zeppelin* Airship
2. 6665 **George (William) Hill** 48, timber merchants labourer, 12 East street, Church street, Drypool [died 6 June]   *do.   do.*
3. 6666 **Jane Hill** 45, wife of the above, 12 East street [died 6 June]   *do.   do.*
4. 6667 **Eliza Slade** 54, widow of George Slade, a fisherman, 4 Walters Terrace, Waller street [died 6 June]   *do.   do.*
5. 6668 **Florence White** 30, wife of Thomas White, 3 Walters Terrace, Waller street [died 6 June]   *do.   do.*

Hull Coroner's Inquest 8 June:
6. 6669 **George Isaac White** 3, son of Thomas White, a dock labourer 3 Walters Terrace, Waller street [died 6 June]   *do.   do.*
7. 6670 **Alfred Matthews** 50, boiler maker, 11 Walters Terrace, Waller street [died 6 June]   *do. do.*
8. 6671 **William Walker** 62, tanner's labourer, 2 St. Thomas Terrace, Campbell street [died 6 June]   *do.   do.*
9. 6672 **Alice Priscilla Walker** 30, daughter of the above, 2 St. Thomas Terrace, Campbell street [died 6 June]   *do.   do.*
10. 6673 **Norman Mullins** 10, son of John William Mullins, a grocer, 39 Blanket Row, Queen street [died at the Infirmary 7 June]   *do.   do.*
11. 6674 **George Mullins** 15, ditto, [died at the Infirmary 7 June]   *do.   do.*
12. 6675 **Emma Pickering**, about 68 years, wife of George Pickering, police constable, 2 Sarah Ann Terrace, Porter street [died at the Infirmary 7 June] *do.   do.*
13. 6676 **Georgina Cunningham** 27, wife of Walter Cunningham, a coal heaver, 22 Edwins Place, Porter street [died 6 June] *do.   do.*

14. 6677 **Edward Jordan** 10, son *of* Edward Jordan, a boiler maker, 11 East street, Church street, Drypool [died 6 June] *do.   do.*

15. 6678 **William Watson** 67, Tram car painter, 21 Edwins Place, Porter street [died 6 June]   *do. do.*

16. 6679 **Annie Watson**, about 58 years, wife of the above 21 Edwins Place [died 6 June]   *do. do.*

17. 6680 **Violet Richardson** 8, daughter of Maurice Richardson, a driver, Royal Fortress Artillery (rullyman), 50 South Parade [died 6 June] *do.   do.*

18. 6681 **Millicent Walker** 17, daughter of William Walter Walker, a tanner's labourer, 2 St. Thomas Terrace, Campbell street [died 6 June] *do. do.*

19. 6682 **Tom [Wood] Stamford** 46, 6 Blanket Row, a lodging house deputy [died 7 June in Naval Hospital] Described as porter in burial register, New Hedon road cemetery; see Dixon ,p.9.[32]

Hull Coroner's Inquest 9 June:
20. 6683 **Ellen Temple** 50, wife of James Temple, a Railway Police Sergeant 20 St. James Square, St. James *street* [Died 8 June] *Fatty degeneration of the heart, syncope. Accelerated by shock of German Zeppelin air raid (P.M.)*

21. 6684 **Elizabeth Pickard Foreman** 39, wife of George Washington Foreman, a general dealer, 37 Walker *street* [died 7 June]   *Valvular disease of the heart. Syncope. Accelerated by shock of German Zeppelin air raid(P.M.)*

22. 6685 **Hannah Mitchell** 42, spinster & housekeeper, 5 Alexandra Terrace, Woodhouse street [died 7 June]   *Fatty degeneration of heart. Cardiac failure do. do. as above (P.M.)*

23. 6686 **Sarah Ann Scott** 36, wife of George William Scott, oil mill labourer, 8 The Poplars, Durham street [Died 7 June] *Fatty degeneration of the heart. Cardiac failure (P.M.)* [aneurism according to burial book of Old Hedon road cemetery; see Dixon, p.7]

24. 6688 **Johanna Harman** 67, wife of Charles Harman, a master mariner, 93 Arundel street [died 7 June*] Fatty degeneration of heart. Syncope accelerated by shock of German Zeppelin air raid (P.M.)*

These are the names found in the post-war descriptions of the air-raids in the Hull newspapers and the *Yorkshire Post*. The former also mention an unidentified woman found in the ruins of Edwin Davis's drapery but this cannot be matched to any record in the coroners 'Inquisitions' book and must therefore qualify as a war time 'myth'.[33]

Related deaths:
Hull Coroner's Inquest 14 June
25. 6728 **Jane Ann Booth** 51, wife of James William Booth, joiner, 2 Alma street, Church street, Drypool [died 14 June] *Valvular and cardiac disease accelerated by shock of the fear of a Zeppelin air raid (P.M.)*
    Complained of internal pains on hearing the air raid buzzer (false alarm) doctor promised medicine, but died before it arrived (see *Hull Daily Mail* 14 July 1915; Dixon, p.7).

A large number of troops were billeted on Hull and around the Humber region as a defence against possible invasion. Inevitably there were casualties by the misuse or careless handling of firearms. For example, a George Roberts, aged 23 (of Crown street, Batley, a cloth worker in civilian life) died 24 March 1915 'accidentally shot with a rifle in the abdomen'.[34]

A raid on Middlesbrough, claimed in official German reports 8 September 1915, did not actually reach this important port and shipbuilding town:

About eight o'clock in the evening a Zeppelin arrived on the North-East Coast somewhere off Whitby, and later followed a train going towards Loftus. The driver of the train saw the Zeppelin, and when he entered a tunnel between Whitby and Loftus remained therein a while. The Zeppelin, it is thought, then mistook Loftus Road for the railway, and dropped one large bomb, making a big hole in the road, but causing no other damage. Shortly afterwards another bomb knocked down a wall between Loftus and Skinningrove. Altogether seven or eight bombs were dropped. The total extent of the damage is stated to be under £100.[35]

****

9a. Zeppelin L11, showing the two gondolas for the crew. Directly above the forward one, perched on top of the envelope is the very exposed gunner's position. Bombed Hull in the second and third raids 6/7 March and 5 April, 1916. (Zeppelin Museum, Friedrichshafen).

9b. Zeppelin L11, inside the control gondola. Along with two crewmen the commander (Viktor Schütze or Freiherr Horst von Buttlar?) checks his chart (Zeppelin Museum, Friedrichshafen).

HULL: Second Zeppelin raid Sunday and Monday 5/6 March 1916, the 'Snowy night raid', L14 Kapitanleutnant Alois Böcker and L11, Kapitanleutnant Horst von Buttlar; previously thought to have been under the command of Korvettenkapitan Viktor Schütze (figs.9a,b).[36]
Hull Coroner's Inquest 7 March
1. 6975 **Edward Cook** 38, general labourer, 33 St. Luke street, Porter street [died 6 March] *Fatty degeneration of the heart, syncope and accelerated by shock from a German air raid (P.M.)*
2. 6976 **John Longstaff** 71, retired loco engine driver, 6 Williams Place, Upper Union street [died 6 March] *do. do. (P.M.)*
3. 6977 **Lottie Ingamells** 28, spinster, daughter of Joseph Ingamells, a waiter, 8 The Avenue, Linnaeus street [died 6 March] *Injuries sustained by the explosion of bombs discharged by a German Zeppelin air ship*
4. 6978 **Edward Slip** 45, refreshment house keeper, 23 Queen street, Market Place [died 6 March] *do. do.*
5. 6979 **Edward Ledner** 89, retired merchant seaman, Almshouse [Trinity House], Carr Lane [died 6 March] *do. do.*
6. 6980 **Frank [William Robert] Cattle** 8, son of Robert Cattle, fish fryer, 50 Little Humber street [died at Queen street 6 March] *do. do. (P. M.)*
7. 6981 **James William Collinson** 65, dock labourer, 14 Johns Place, Regent street [died 6 March] *Injuries sustained by the explosion of bombs discharged by a German Zeppelin airship*
8. 6982 **George Henry Youell** 40, a dry dock labourer, 4 Post Office Entry, High street/Blackfriargate [died 6 March outside Infirmary] *do. do.*

9. 6983 **Charlotte Naylor**, about 36 years, wife of Edwin Naylor, a dock labourer 32 Collier street, Brook street [died 6 March]   *do. do.*

10. 6984 **Ruby [Mary] Naylor** 8, daughter of the above [died 6 March]   *do.   do.*

11. 6985 **Annie Naylor** 6, daughter of the above   [died at Infirmary 6 March] *do.   do.*

12. 6986 **Edward Naylor** 4, son of the above, 32 Collier street, Brook street [died 6 March]   *do do.*

13. 6987 **Jeffrey Naylor** 2, son of the above, 32 Collier street, Brook street [died 6 March]   *do. do.*

14. 6988 **John Smith** 30, dock labourer, 2 Queens Alley, Blackfriargate [died at Queen street 6 March]   *do.   do.*

15. 6989 **James Pattison** 68, a chimney sweep, 39B Regent street, Anlaby road [died 6 March at Naval Hospital] *do.   do.*

16. 6990 **Martha Rebeca Ingamells** 35, spinster, daughter of Joseph Ingamells, a waiter, 8 The Avenue, Linnaeus street [died 6 March at Naval Hospital] *Injuries sustained by the explosion of bombs discharged by a German Zeppelin airship.*

17. 6991 **Ethel Mary Ingamells** 33, 8 The Avenue, Linnaeus street [died 6 March at Naval Hospital]   *do. do.*

Hull Coroner's Inquest 18 September 1916:

18. 7168 **William Jones** 80, merchant seaman (retired), Room 19 Trinity House Almshouse, Posterngate [died here 17 September 1916] *Injuries sustained by the explosion of a bomb discharged by a Zeppelin airship on 6 March last. Shock. Heart failure (P.M.)*
Sustained head injuries in air raid, wound healed but shock caused heart failure. Perhaps had a fall during the raid; there is no indication of a bomb landing in the vicinity of the almshouse adjacent to the Princes dock, though maybe a bomb had fallen in or near the adjoining Princes dock. Details of damage to strategic targets tended to be heavily censored and there is no surviving documentation which gives a clear picture of the impact of bombing on the docks, railways, factories etc. (*Hull Daily Mail* 10 September; see Dixon).

Over in the West Riding, Sheffield was visited by Zeppelin L22, 25/26 September 1916. A devastating raid during which the anti-aircraft guns failed to fire a shot, resulting in 28 dead (9 men, 9 women and 10 children) and 19 injured.

****

The memoir of Bernard Heald, includes a description of the second raid; then aged 13 he was living with his widowed mother at 34 Lee street, Holderness road:

> The fairly lengthy period without any Zeppelin raids came to an end on Sunday, March 5th. It had been snowing intermittently during the day, and by nightfall the countryside was white over. Not long after dark, the ominous notes of the air raid warning buzzers were heard, and for a while nothing more happened. Our family sat around talking, or trying to read by the aid of a couple of candles-mother had turned off the gas - and we were beginning to think that this was another of the warnings without a subsequent raid, when around 9 p.m. we heard the distant, characteristic high-pitched beat of Zeppelin engines. My family and our next door neighbours shared a covered concrete passageway between the houses, and we had agreed to use this as an air raid shelter, so when an alarm sounded, an old carpet was put down and blankets arranged, so that a quick exodus could be made from the houses.
>
> Putting out our candles, we quickly made for the passageway, as the engine beats got louder. A few minutes later, we heard the 'Crump! Crump!' of falling bombs exploding some distance away. After a brief interval, there it was again, and yet again,

with apparently no reply from our anti-aircraft gun on Rose, Downs foundry roof. At the height of the raid our next door neighbour's daughter, a girl of about 17, became hysterical and could not be quietened. At length her father sought to give her a swig from a bottle of brandy which he kept handy, and in the darkness and confusion mistook my sister Dorothy for her, and tried to force the brandy down Dorothy's throat. She screamed and fought against these attentions and 'Dad' kept saying, 'Now, now, dear, this will help you, now be a good girl and drink up. Come on, dear, it will do you good.' Pandemonium reigned for some minutes until things were sorted out! Later on, we had some good laughs over this incident, and Dorothy's leg was pulled on many occasions. In fact, I can recall my mother and sister being almost hysterical themselves as I mimicked the role of the good neighbour with the aid of a lemonade bottle and Dorothy's unwilling mouth!

However, back to the more serious matter of the air raid. At last, the sound of explosions ceased, and I remember stealing out into the snow-covered street, and seeing dimly against the star-lit sky, a cigar-shaped raider making for the coast.

After what seemed an eternity, the welcome note of the air raid relief sirens was heard, and we rather wearily made our way back into the house again, where mother made us a cup of tea [this was about 2a.m.].[37]

****

During February Margaret Strickland-Constable was in London, as a volunteer serving in the canteens at Woolwich Arsenal, both in the tailoring 'shop' and the cordite 'shop'. She possibly also worked for a time in the censorship office:

Mar. 5th Zepp. Raid at Hull. Beverley, Grimsby. F, travelling from London, was due at Hull at 11 p.m., but did not arrive till 6 a.m. Queen street wrecked (fig.9a,b,c). **Windows of Holy Trinity broken, glass roof of station broken, a bomb in a field**

9c. Queen street, Hull, after second raid, 5 March 1916; on the corner is the Moors and Robson's public house 'Golden Lion'; photograph by Marcus Barnard, from a souvenir booklet, Hull Daily News (Hull Museums).

close to Hedon, 2 bombs in Beverley (harmless) - flare dropped in the garden at Heighington.

[back at the Arsenal. March 8th]

****

HULL: Third Zeppelin raid L11 Oberleutnant zur See Hoorst von Buttlar, previously thought to have been Korvettenkapitan Viktor Schütze[38]. Wednesday 5 April 1916 :

Hull Coroner's Inquest April 3 1916

1. 7017 **Ada Ellen Redfern** 23,wife of John Henry Redfern, Private in the 7th or 8th E.Y. Regiment(a bricklayer), 5 Sarah Terrace, Courtney street[39] (died 2 April 1916) *Shock from fear of a German Zeppelin Air Raid* (P.M.)

[**Jessie Matthews** 2 months, daughter of Charles Matthews, soldier, 11 Cotton Terrace, Barnsley street buried Old Hedon road cemetery (died of convulsions 4 April; see Dixon p.8). This infant is recorded as a casualty in the newspapers but in the burial records her date of death is given as 4 April, the day before the raid! There was no coroner's inquest.]

A post card image of a Zeppelin caught in the searchlights, entitled 'TRAPPED, WEDNESDAY NIGHT,5 April,1916' was produced by Smith's Publishing, 118 Hessle Road, Hull(fig.10).[40] Another postcard, H. Miles, Printer, Charles street, reproduces some verses condemning the attack on defenceless civilians, entitled 'The defeat of the Zeppelin 5 April 1916'(fig.11).[41]

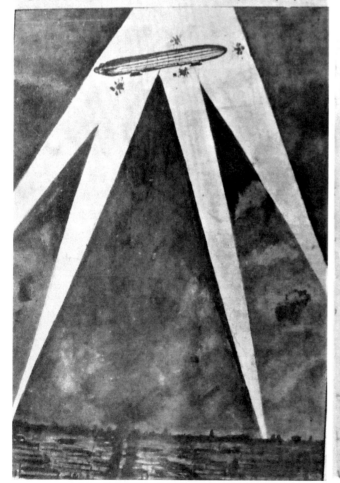

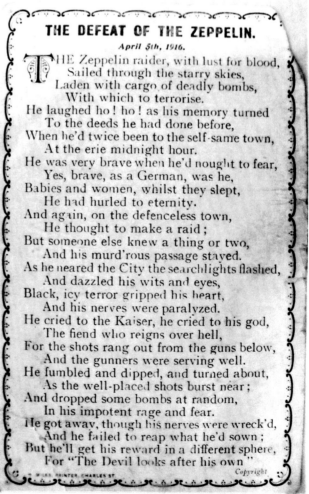

10. Postcard of Zeppelin caught in the searchlights over Hull, 5 April 1916; a drawing, not a photograph (Hull Museums).

11. Postcard with verses on the raid by Zeppelin L11, 5 April 1916; it was not brought down but hastily departed in the face of sustained gunfire.

L11, Korvettenkapitan Schütze was driven off after dropping four bombs, the first in Portobello street; the airship was picked up by the searchlights and came under immediate anti-aircraft fire. The Hull newspapers (though not allowed to say at which town the raid had taken place!) gave a rousing account and George Thorp records in his diary:

> I saw that the [searchlight] beams of different localities, Endike Lane, Liverpool Street and Marfleet had caught Herr Zeppelin in one common focus and were hammering at him with the long range guns as hard as they could go. The scream of the missiles as they tore through the air exploding above and below and on each side some bursting very near, but I don't think it was hit, but the Monster which I saw very clearly did not appreciate his very warm reception, for it made off very rapidly in a North Easterly direction.[42]

In the Hull Museum collection is a coloured illustration of a moonlit townscape (apparently London), which has an inscription FIND THE ZEPPELIN. On reversing it an image is revealed of a Zeppelin as though caught in a cone of light (fig.12a,b).[43]. Probably an item given in a newspaper or magazine, though whether during or after the war is not known.

HULL: Fourth Zeppelin raid L24 Kapitänleutnant Robert Koch. Monday and Tuesday 8/9 August 1916:

Hull Coroner's Inquest 9 August:
1. 7136 **Arthur Wilcockson** 86, Calvinist minister, 32 Granville street *Shock through a German Zeppelin air raid on 9th instant*

Hull Coroner's Inquest 10 August:
2. 7137 **Mary Louisa Bearpark** 44, wife of Albert Edward Bearpark, a stevedore, 35 Selby street, Anlaby road   *Injuries sustained by the explosion of bombs discharged by a German Zeppelin on 9th instant*
3. 7138 **John Charles Broadley** 3, son of John Edward Broadley, bricklayer, 4 Rowlands Avenue, Arthur street   *do.   do.*
4. 7139 **Elizabeth Hall** 9, daughter of Alfred Henry Hall, 61 Selby street, Anlaby road, Private, Royal Flying Corps   *do.   do.*
5. 7140 **Emma Louisa Evers** 46, spinster, daughter of Jonathan Evers, 25 Brunswick Avenue, St. Georges road [died at Walliker street (Myton)]   *do.   do.*
6. 7141 **Esther Stobbart** 21, wife of Frank Joseph Stobbart, Sgt. 7833, 3rd E.Y. Regt. (chemists assistant), 13 Henrys Terrace, Wassand street   *shock due to above*

Hull Coroner's Inquest 10 August
{7142 **Elizabeth Jane Bond** 76, 5 Sydney Terrace, Grange street, wife [widow] of James Bond, railway company labourer [died 9 August] *Natural causes. Abscess on brain, apoplexy (P.M.)*

Though listed in the newspapers as a Zeppelin casualty the coroner's record makes no reference to the air raid. After the 8/9 August raid she went outside, fell and sustained head injuries. Taken to the infirmary and died next morning (*Hull Daily Mail* 10 August; see Dixon p.6).}

7. 7143 **Mary Hall** 7, daughter of Alfred Henry Hall, private RFC, 61 Selby street, Anlaby road [died at the infirmary 9 August] *Injuries sustained by the explosion of bombs discharged by a German Zeppelin air ship on 9th instant.*
8. 7144 **Rose Alma Hall** 31, wife of above, 61 Selby street, Anlaby road [died 10 August, at the Naval Hospital]   *do.   do.*

12a, b. FIND A ZEPPELIN..

9. 7145 **Emmie Bearpark** 14, daughter of Albert Edward Bearpark, a stevedore 35 Selby street, Anlaby road [died 9 August at Naval Hospital]   *do.   do.*

Hull Coroner's Inquest 15 August:

10. 7149 **Charles Lingard** 64, a cab driver, 61 Walliker street, Anlaby road [died 14 August] *Fracture of skull consequent upon bombs discharged by a German Zeppelin airship on 9th instant (P.M.).*

{William Clarkson 62, ironmonger, 2 Adderbury Grove, Beverley road, died of heart failure 22 August 1917; possibly death from fear induced by air raid warning buzzer, he is reported as a Zeppelin casualty in the newspapers, but died of heart failure nearly a fortnight after the raid, there was no inquest; see Dixon p.17.}

****

Diary of Margaret Strickland –Constable continued:

> *Aug. 9th* **Motored to Hull to see damage–only 4 houses wrecked. 8 people killed. In Walliker St. we saw 1 house completely wrecked, a large hole in the ground, and every pane of glass broken for several streets around. A few days later we heard that stones had been thrown at the Mayor's windows, & that they had threatened to throw Gen. Ferrier[44] into the harbour if he came into East Hull, and that they all threaten to come out on strike if better protection is not provided.**

The Hull defences were described as one searchlight and a 'pop-gun'; the later being the dummy gun on the Blundell and Spence premises mentioned above. Without the 'eyes' given by radar during the 1939-45 war ground mist had effectively blinded the Hull anti-aircraft gunners and only eight rounds were fired. The poor visibility also prevented aircraft from taking off.

There were guns at Spurn, at Paull, and on the south bank of the Humber but at the beginning of the war none actually within the city. Defence was purely passive, relying on blackout and the silencing of church bells, public clocks and any other source of loud noises and light. Most available guns had been sent to the Western Front to prevent the German advance and there was a desperate shortage for home defence. As the threat to London became more apparent the capital claimed priority, both as the seat of government and as the hub of empire trade. Any raid resulting in significant damage was a propaganda coup for the Germans, and London also became the target for the *Gotha* bombers, a large biplane with a wingspan of 78 feet, and the enormous *Giants* with a wingspan of over 138 feet!

There was a constant juggling with scarce resources, and guns and searchlights were moved from town to town in anticipation of a raid. As a result individual municipal authorities were never certain whether there was going to be adequate protection available when required. Anti-aircraft guns did slowly become more plentiful and more effective, and with the use of incendiary and explosive bullets by aircraft the airships were forced to fly ever higher for their own protection. As a result it became more and more difficult to concentrate bombs on a specific target and do significant damage.

Airship L9 flew up the Humber estuary intending to attack Hull but because of mist and a faulty rudder the pilot lost his way and overshot his target by some 20 miles to the west and dropped his bombs over Goole:[45]

Shortly after eleven o'clock on the night of August 9, 1916, a Zeppelin carried out a raid on Goole. The airship made a swift passage over the town, but within the space of five minutes over 50 bombs were dropped.

Thirteen persons were killed[46]. Their names were:-Annie Goodall (74) widow, 4, Bromley's Yard; Violet Stainton (18) 30, George Street; Agnes Pratt (36), and Margaret Pratt (9 months) Bromley's Yard; Grace Woodhall, 5 Bromley's Yard; Annie Elizabeth Woodhall (3); James Carroll (32), Mary Carroll (32), Alice Carroll (4), and Gladys Carroll (3), Back North Street; Sarah Acaster (65), Kezia Acaster (32), and Sarah Ann Acaster (34), 2 Cottam Street.

The names of the injured were:-
William Rigg (50) and Mary Rigg, Bromley's Yard; Margaret Barber, Back North Street; Alice Smith [dead according to Butler, see below] *and Dinah Goulders, 47 George Street; Nellie Hattersley, 28 George Street, Sarah Ann Woodhall, 5 Bromley's Yard; Alice Harrison and Florence Harrison, Belle Vue Terrace* [these last two died, making a total of 16, see below].

It is thought that the Zeppelin was guided by flare from the engine of a goods train, for as this was passing over the Hook Bridge, the searchlight of the airship flashed out overhead, and immediately a number of bombs were dropped obviously with the intention of destroying this important railway span over the Ouse. Happily all the projectiles missed their mark, and plunged harmlessly into the river and a wheat-field about 20 yards away.

The airship travelling at great speed, pursued a course over the centre of the town, unsuccessfully attempting to wreck in its passage the Water Tower and the gasometers. When it was over the residential part of Goole an explosive bomb was dropped on a house in Cottam Street, wrecking the premises and killing a widow named, named Acaster, and her two daughters. An extensive block of slum property near to the docks, which is bounded by George Street, Ouse Street and North Street, and contains an area called Bromley's Yard, bore the brunt of the havoc which the Zeppelin caused. In this part also were the other victims. The four members of the Carroll family had gone to bed, when a powerful bomb pierced the roof, the ensuing explosion demolishing the house and those immediately on each side, and killing the occupants. In Aire Street which runs alongside of the Aldam Dock, a bomb struck a pile of logwood, and the force of the explosion blew in the windows of a row of shops. The Lowther Hotel, a famous old coaching house at the end of this thoroughfare was badly damaged, all the windows being broken, the doors forced in, and the interior fittings torn from the walls. The Zeppelin hovered for a moment or two over the Stanhope Dock, and dropped two incendiary bombs, which struck warehouses but caused very little damage. Two large Dutch merchant steamers in the dock narrowly escaped being hit. The airship then swung round in a north-easterly direction and disappeared.[47]

A letter from a Mr. West, a shipping clerk, to his daughter apparently enjoying the summer holiday break from her studies at Leeds Training College, is a lively eyewitness account. It is especially interesting in giving details of damage to docks and railways, which were the true targets of German bombs, no mention of which was allowed during the war and not usually considered of interest after hostilities ceased:

'Steam Ship Manager   *Telegraphic address 'Despatch Goole'*
    G.W. Winterbottom, Goole   Nat. Telephone Nos.26,40 & 77.
                    Lancashire and Yorkshire Railway
                        Goole Steam Shipping
                        Goole, Aug. 12th, 1915

My child, yours is to hand. Mum did not wish to spoil your outing, and so did not mention anything to cause anxiety. We did not expect anything would be allowed in the papers, <u>so soon</u>, by the censor. Enjoy your holiday, while you have the opportunity. Well now! The zeps came at 1.15 p.m. [Tuesday crossed out] Monday. Hook bridge, got the first. They tried hard for bridge, dropping 3 bombs, but all missed- they are all at the bottom of the Ouse. Many dropped between bridge and Goole, but, striking soft soil, never exploded- three were dug out of the barley field at Kingsway end, they passed our house to the police station: some took 2 men to lift them. One fell at Jessies's back, onto the Kelsey's; <u>that</u> didn't explode, luckily; the next struck a house in Axholme street, passing thro' roof, & I can tell you the deep booming roar woke me,& our room was one red glare-all Shuffelton seemed to be ablaze.⁴⁸ Ma thought it was thunder, & lightning. I kept quite cool and resigned - it was an incendiary bomb, but the fire was put out. The next fell thro roof of Mrs. Acaster, the stone house, next to our butcher's - four were sat at supper & 3 were killed: Mrs. + 2 daughters, a visitor escaping [unhurt crossed out]. Another fell just opposite this one, the other side of Victoria street, next to Clarkson's shop & next to where Mrs. Ellis went to live; it crashed thro roof, & was an incendiary, but fire was put out. I have had a piece of it in my hand. Walker, Hook road was repairing roof yesterday. <u>Then</u> came some demons. One fell in George street (Back)- 3 houses had wall blown out into the lane, & beds, bairns, bolsters & pictures after them.4 killed.

Roof crashed down on Thursday m[ornin]g. Pa, Ma,2 children- Mr. Gunnee carried girl out, all flesh, of one leg torn away- next he fetched a young baby, but the sight finished him; he was done----sick---he went away ---to vomit. Had it been a man, he says he would not care. Next fell in Ouse, (Back) near T.K. Wilson's baker. Hole in wall, drive horse & cart thro'- floors are all down in the cellar, furniture just a pile of ruin, pictures hang akimbo. Next a beast came, for destruction to property, tho not to life, fortunately. It struck the Quay wall, just opposite Adam street end. Stone blocks 2 feet thick, were splintered, and the solid masonry under them. Docks hydraulic pipes broken, log wood sent flying. Railway wagons derailed & smashed to pieces - Lowther hotel hasn't a window left, all blown out (or in) woodwork included & so is all Aire street, Hoppers, Makintosh, Murdock, right to Armitages & Timm's.

Our office end windows broken & so are Brook's Bank. All are now white boards, nailed up. Next fell on our Hamburg ⁴⁹shed; it smoldered [sic] some hours and then burst into flame, at 6.00 a.m.. Most is destroyed, shed & contents. Another fell near, into a wooden shed, & blew it to pieces, scattering goods, slates & planks in all directions. Next fell on the coal sidings, just off Bridge Street. Could you have seen result, you would know what a crater is; it made one. A loaded truck, 14 tons, was shoved off the line, <u>both</u> rails broken & bent inward, aye and split lengthwise, I <u>saw</u> them. An N.E.R. truck knocked into fragments, & one of our butter vans smashed. Steel springs & thick iron gease boxes (where the axle turns in) broken like match wood. More fell near Alum works, where similar craters were made, & minor damage done. We shall never know how many were dropped, some are at the bottom of the dock, I have talked to a man who was in a small boat, at the time, near a coal hoist; he did not know where to turn for safety, they seemed everywhere, one passed close to him, into the water. But you should have seen the fugitives fleeing. Mount Pleasant was swarming; swarming. The Harrison girls slept on the bare ground, there, See a barefoot woman, only nightdress on, a baby in her arms, & 2 children pulling at her.

Midnight- yes! 20ᵗʰ century kultur⁵⁰ and all up to the knees in wet & field soil. We had had down pour all morning. Airmyn and Rawcliffe roads were alive, all night. All flocked out, too, on Tuesday, at dusk, but better prepared. Men and women, bairns⁵¹ & baskets, chairs & stools: aye & even beds were taken out to field & hedge side, road and lane, seeking safety =14 were killed but 2 more children, girls died in the hospital, y' day-

inquest is on, this mg: funeral tomorrow. There are some 36 unexploded bombs at Police station, I am told=and are to be on view this afternoon}
Later- It would seem Mrs. Acaster's visitor was hurt, and is since dead - that brings it to 17 victims; she was from London, & a relative of Mrs. Ramsay's & had gone to the Acaster's for the night, so she had just walked into it, showing that we know not what a day may bring forth-what is to be, will be. Mrs Acaster is to be buried today ; the rest tomorrow in common grave; Compton Rickett takes the expense.[52] Mrs. A has a son in the Dardanelles - but I can't tell you all = Invite your friend to Goole, we can make her welcome; mother will be pleased to see her, faithfully 'Pa.'[53]

Photographs of the damage to the Lowther Hotel and Back North Street have been published[54] and a mention of the raid appears in the memoir of the actress Evelyn Laye (1900-1996). Aged 15 she had made her stage debut at the Theatre Royal, Brighton, in the same month:

Daddy was with me when we played Goole in a bitterly cold theatre with dressing rooms upstairs in a loft, and a Zeppelin raid caught us. I drank my first whisky that night administered to me by my Father as the best air-raid precaution he knew. he then tucked me up on a horse-hair sofa, covered me with his coat and sat guard by me all night while the crashing of the German bombs shook the dark frightened little town. [55]

As always with the casualties of Zeppelin raids there is confusion over the precise number of dead and injured. The contemporary account in the local newspaper gives the number of 16 killed, the tally subsequently repeated, including nine women and six children, including two girls who died in hospital. The wounded numbered five men, seven women, and several children.[56] A more detailed description of the raid and an account of the coroner's inquest appeared soon after the war ended. Sixteen is given as the total number of dead but the names of only 15 people are listed: 1. James Carroll, a marine fireman (31), his wife 2. Mary Carroll (30), and two children 3. Alice Carroll (3) 4.Gladys Carroll (2) at 6 (?) Back North street; 5. Hannah [elsewhere named Annie] Goodall (74), 4 Bromley's Yard (4), a widow, mother of Frank Stainton, a boatman (74), and 6. Her granddaughter Violet Stainton, 30 George Street, in domestic service, daughter of Mrs Fanny Stainton, wife of a boatman (18), died on Tuesday morning; 7. Agnes Pratt (36), at 3 (?) Bromley's Yard, wife of William Pratt, a merchant seaman, and daughter of Mrs. Selina Hattersley by a former husband and 8. her daughter Margaret Pratt (9 months); 9. Grace Woodal [or Woodhall] (31), 5 Bromley's Yard died in a cab on the way to hospital and 10. her daughter Annie Elizabeth Woodall (3), 5 Bromley's Yard (?) the wife and daughter of Private Larkin Woodall of the 3/5 K.O.Y.L.I; 11. Sarah Acaster (65), died soon after arrival at hospital, widow of Benjamin Acaster, master stone mason, and her unmarried daughters, 12. Keziah Acaster, a spinster (32), and 13. Sarah Ann Acaster (34), spinster, 2 Cottam street (the latter manageress of a shop selling toys and sweets) 14. Beatrice Alice Harrison (6), Belle Vue Terrace, died early Wednesday afternoon, and 15. Florrie Harrison (4) daughters of Beatrice Lavinia Harrison, wife of a marine fireman, George Frederick Harrison. [57]

Susan Butler gives Alice Smith, a domestic servant, as deceased, but this may not have been the case, and the sixteenth victim was more likely the unnamed visitor at the Acasters[58],or if West was correct there were 17 victims in all not 16.

****

Zeppelins passed over the coast near Hornsea and Bridlington on several occasions in the ensuing weeks and bombs had been dropped in Lincolnshire but no further raids on Hull till 2

September; but no bombs were dropped on that occasion and there are no entries in Margaret Strickland-Constable's diary.

Nine people were killed at York in a raid on 2 May 1916 [59] and a letter reveals the panic that ensued:

> *I have seen a bit in my time and I have a bit of nerve but I never want to see any more of this. Women and children running about screaming and in their nightgowns--- it has unnerved everybody. People are today walking about with a vacant, potty stare on their faces.*[60]

The history of Pocklington Grammar School, some 13 miles from York, records:

> *In these days of lightning bomber raids it is strange to remember the threatening hum of the comparatively slow airship, faintly seen above like a colossal cigar, avoiding moonlit nights*[61] *and cruising about to find a well lighted town. Decoys were lit then as later*[62] *and a fire purposely made on Barmby Common saved York Minster but caused the demolition of a pig-sty. The airship's engines so alarmed the Pocklington townsfolk that they sent a message to the headmaster asking him to quieten the boys' voices for fear they should guide the Zeppelin crew into dropping their load!*[63]

All the principal stained glass windows had been removed from York Minster and put into safe storage, replaced with plain glass until after the war. There was a degree of awareness by the government and the military authorities of the likelihood of air raids. At first this was notional but the dropping of bombs on Antwerp in late August 1914 during the German advance through Belgium, gave an insight into the effects of aerial bombardment.

The English service chiefs, aware of the potential dangers of the Zeppelin, made a number of 'pre-emptive strikes' before a single enemy airship had been seen over Britain. A poverty of home defences certainly made offence the best form of defence. An attack was made on Dusseldorf, 8 October 1914, destroying a Zeppelin in its hangar and the next month, 21 November, the Zeppelin factory itself, at Friedrichshafen was bombed by Avro 504 biplanes. A total of six Zeppelins were destroyed in the first year of the war by carrying the fight to the enemy.

Some at least of the civilian population, those with technical and specialist knowledge, had an inkling of what might be coming their way, but for the overwhelming majority it was beyond their comprehension and imagining. H.G. Wells in his *War in the air* of 1908 wrote of an apocalyptic world war with the collapse of civilisation following the destruction made by great fleets of German airships. Most readers however no doubt regarded this as science fiction in the same vein as the Martian invasion described in his *War of the Worlds* (1897), rather than a speculation or prediction of what technological advances might make possible.

Even as the war started the authorities made no attempt to educate the public and prepare them for the possibility of aerial attack. The actuality of a raid, late at night, with initially no means of retaliation, and the sight of these monstrous craft, some 400 feet in length, deliberately manoeuvring into position and dropping their lethal loads of incendiary and highly explosive bombs must have been truly terrifying. Aerial attack was an entirely new and shocking experience and it was aimed at a population totally unprepared for being the direct targets of an enemy up in the sky. There had not been any significant number of casualties from military activity on native soil since the Civil War in the 17th century, and the safety and comfort of civilian life was suddenly shattered.

****

In the south of England there had been some successes, *L15* was brought down in the sea south-east of the Kentish Knock lightship, 1 April 1916, (see below), and later the same year 3 September, with the aid of the new incendiary bullet, the airship *Schütte-Lanz SL II* was shot down in flames over Cuffley, Herts. Flying his B.E.2c Lieutenant William Leefe Robinson emptied several drums of ammunition into the envelope and the airship fell from the skies in flames. As well as being equipped with bullets that could ignite the flammable hydrogen in the gas bags he was also using a new gun sight made by the eminent London gunmakers, James Purdey and Sons. The Norman sight was devised by Professor Norman of Cambridge and developed by Ernest Lawrence in the Purdey workshop.[64]

This airship was the first to be brought down on dry land in Britain, and though popularly referred to as a Zeppelin was actually a Schütte-Lanz craft, an airship of a different design operated by the German army. The true Zeppelin generally sent on raids was manned by members of the German Imperial navy. The successful downing of an airship was a great morale booster and after its loss no more of its type were seen over Britain. Leefe-Robinson became a national hero, was awarded the Victoria Cross but subsequently died in the influenza epidemic of 1919.

Pursuit of the SL11 was followed by excited onlookers as it flew across the metropolis and into the home counties. After coming to earth its remains were assailed by hundreds of souvenir hunters, one of these being the Hull M.P. Sir Mark Sykes who had driven from London, where he worked at the War Office, to gather mementoes for his children. His letter home, occasionally breaking into mock cockney, includes sketches of the airship's last moments:[65]

9, Buckingham Gate S.W.

Sunday Aug 3 1916

I have foregone my week end and have been rewarded - at 2.15 a.m. I was aroused from a dream of Lloyd George moving all our furniture & throwing it down stairs by finding that shells were bursting in both sides of the house say about 1½ miles away, out of your window I only saw shells, but I crossed to the other side & saw a Zep very clearly with shells bursting near it, in about 5 min it moved off due north and disappeared, so I went back to watch the bombardment on the cathedral side, suddenly the sky from the north began to light up until it was like day light just after sun rise only bright red, I ran back to my room only it was quite dark again- only every where you could hear little distant cheers the light lasted by my calculation about 35 seconds-a lot of excited specials came running down the street and the bugles blew the alarm in the barracks, and firing on all sides ceased at 2.30.- Next morning I saw Buckeley and he suggested we go search for the destroyed Zep: that was the light- so after lunch off to the tube and so to Finsbury park with W.O. passes, at Finsbury park the station was crowded with delighted people, the train crammed –so into a guards van with 15 people including 6 extra police, by the time we got to Cuffley there were 40 in the guards van, children, Mrs Nuggens clerks, farmers all agog with joy-
Wish the ole Kaiser coud 'ear us talk! – Terrified har we?- we mus' write to Tom at Sally onoka bout vis! etc. etc. At Cuffley it was Goodwood on the big day[66], cars & crowds, bycycles, motors, dog carts, vans full of girls and men and converging streams of people on foot, all in the highest spirits, I cannot estimate crowds but every road was blocked & people were pouring over the fields, and remember every platform of the 12 stations between Finsbury Park and Cuffley had been crowded - so to a little field where some 200 Scots Guards held the ground, and in the midst of it the wreckage –the Zep had been dealt with thus [followed by 4 sketches (figs.13 a,b,c]
*So you see it telescoped on to itself[67] and occupied in consequence extraordinarily little space instead of **A** [sketch] it was **B**[sketch]- much was fished out of the wreckage one*

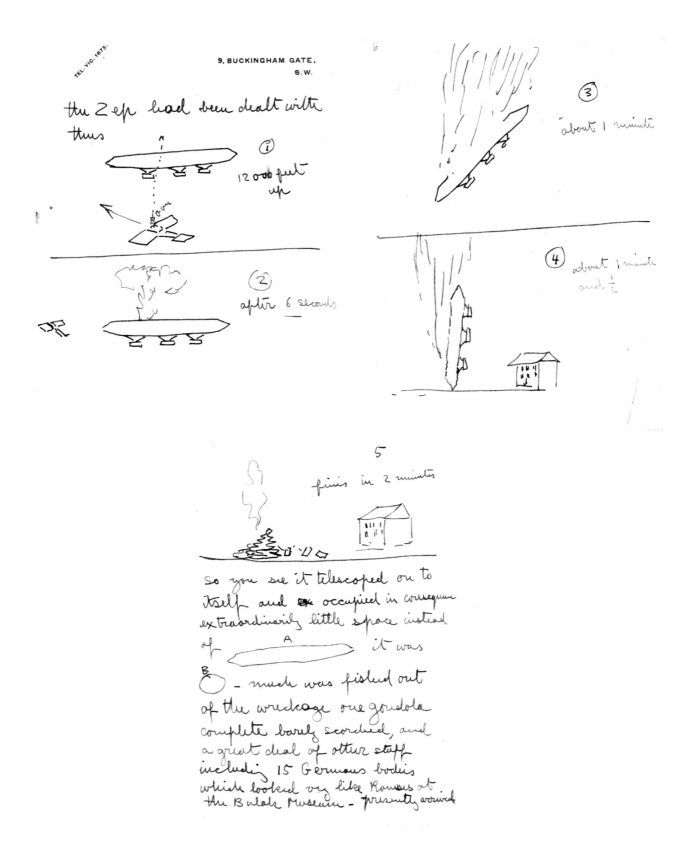

13 a, b, c. Sketches of the demise of airship SL11 over Cuffley, in a letter from Mark Sykes M.P. to his wife.

gondola complete barely scorched, and a great deal of other stuff including 15 Germans bodies which looked like Rameses at the Bulak Museum[68]- presently arrived a party of Cambon,[69] General Paget, lady Paget, McKenna, Mrs McKenna, young Nicolson & his wife[70] and Dr. Ross - loud cheers for Cambon, and Buckeley and I finding ourselves benighted begged a lift and so home in a swift motor- The boy Robinson who bagged the Zep who will be famous - was so excited after he had succeeded he sent all the signals wrong- viz! 'failed'- 'try again'- 'going on further'-

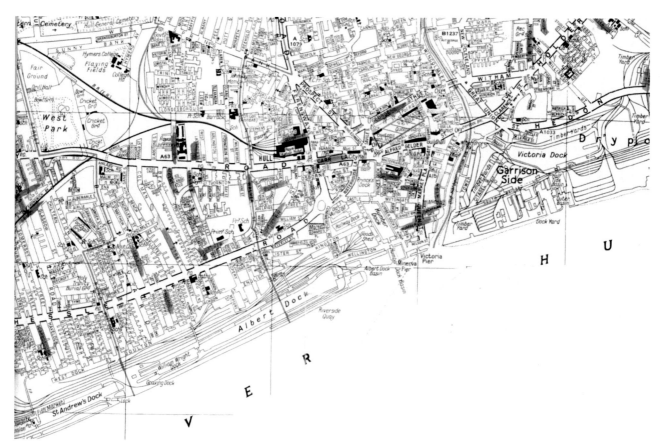

14. Map, the areas suffering major damage are shaded. Clearly the intended targets were the town docks and nearby warehouses and railways storage areas, but many bombs, both H.E. and incendiaries, landed on adjacent housing.

15. Pen and ink drawing by George Dancey following the downing of Zeppelin L15 off the Thames estuary, 1 April 1916..

A most interesting afternoon I think- don't you- I am sending each of the children a piece of Zep but they must keep them.[71]

Throughout the entire war not a single airship was brought down over Yorkshire and indeed only one was destroyed in the north of England as a whole. On the night of 27/28 November 1916 Second Lieutenant Ian Vernon Pyott in a BE2c from Cramlington, Northumberland, chased the L34 from West Hartlepool over the coast, firing incendiary bullets, and the blazing wreck fell into the sea off the Tees, all the crew died.[72] In the north there were insufficient anti-aircraft guns and a shortage of the more up to date and powerful pursuit aircraft which might have been expected to get within effective shooting distance of the high-flying airships.

If we plot the main locations where bombs landed and caused damage to property, and loss of life and injury, it is clear that the attackers were aiming for the docks and railways. Inevitably anyone living adjacent to these strategic targets was in danger and working class housing in some of the poorest parts of the city was severely affected (fig.14). The spartan living conditions of many of

16a. Gold medal given to anti-aircraft crews involved in the destruction of L15: PRESENTED BY THE LORD MAYOR COLONEL SIR CHARLES WAKEFIELD.

16b. Reverse of gold medal: L15 WELL HIT MARCH 31ST-APRIL 1ST 1916. Inscribed CORPL C. BROWN.

their inhabitants is highlighted by the photograph of the interior of a house in Great Thornton street, after the first raid in June 1915 (fig.7b).

Because of strict censorship there are no details from official sources of what level of destruction occurred on the railways, docks and associated warehouses and storage areas, except that in the first raid Hewitt's timber yard was set on fire and the site photographed by Charles Turner. The letter by a shipping clerk to his daughter, describing the only attack on Goole (9 August 1915), would suggest that the effects might well have been considerable (see above). It would however have been necessary for the aerial bombing to have been more frequent and sustained to achieve any long-term diminution of the city's contribution to the war effort.

Of the total of eight attacks from June 1915 to May 1918, the last four (1917-18) were ineffectual, indicative of the Zeppelins being forced to operate at a greater height, both to avoid increased anti-aircraft fire and the pursuit aircraft that were now equipped with explosive and incendiary bullets. The first raid resulted in the most casualties but there was then a gap of nine months before the second in March 1916. There was a total of three raids in 1916, each of which resulted

16c. Watercolour by J.S. Riches, 1916, depicting rescue of the crew of Zeppelin L15 by men of the Hull armed trawler Olivine.

17. A Bruce Bairnsfather cartoon, 1918; his famous character 'Old Bill' occupying a shell hole on the western front and thinking of the folks back home..

in loss of life and destruction of buildings, then there was a gap of a whole year before the next aerial attack in September 1917.

In the best British tradition the Zeppelin menace inspired a number of cartoons. A pen and ink drawing by George Dancey, cartoonist and mural designer, shows a soldier alongside a tweedy gentleman, John Bull inscribed on his hat, holding a smoking shotgun, and a Zeppelin falling out of the sky (fig.15). This is evidently the L15 brought down in the sea off the Thames estuary, soon after midnight, 30 March 1916, its crew were rescued by an armed trawler, the *Olivine*, H849, of Hull. Finished off by air attack the craft was initially damaged by anti-aircraft fire and a privately made medal, in 9 carat gold, was given by Sir Charles Wakefield, Lord Mayor of London, to some three hundred men of the A-A crews defending the metropolis[73](fig.16a,b).

Bruce Bairnsfather, the soldier cartoonist of the 1914-18 war, using his celebrated character 'old Bill', demonstrates the awareness of the men in the trenches of the dangers of the Zeppelins to their wives and families at home (fig. 17). An altogether more dramatic imagining by a Russian artist of 1914 shows a bevy of biplanes attacking an airship caught in the searchlights and men tumbling from a disintegrating aircraft.

The prolific Hull cartoonist Ern Shaw normally associated with sporting subjects and gentle social satire did produce at least one political piece, on behalf of the Labour Party, Transport House. It

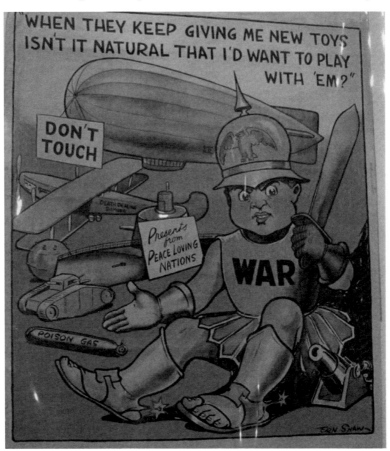

18. Rare (unique?) political piece by Hull cartoonist Ern Shaw, the 'Toys of war' (Private collection).

shows a baby armed with a sword, wearing a pickelhaube, and surrounded by his 'toys of war' including an airship, bomber aircraft, submarine, tank, mine, artillery gun and cylinder of poison gas (fig.18).[74]

In the early days of the war, before strict censorship was imposed, reports of Zeppelin attacks in British newspapers were often repeated in the Dutch press, the Netherlands was neutral, enabling the German war office to assess the effectiveness or otherwise of a particular attack. Without radar and the modern aids which accurately fix position the Zeppelin pilots often did not know where their bombs had landed until an attack was reported in the neutral press. German sources were also quoted in the Dutch newspapers, and a German naval telegram, claimed that:

> On approaching the British coast bombs were lavishly dropped on enemy outpost vessels.
> The naval forces and land batteries fired briskly at our airships, which replied with well directed volleys upon Spurn Head battery.
> Towards two o'clock in the morning large quantities of explosives were dropped on Hull and good incendiary and destructive effect were observed. The airships dropped bombs on Lincoln with observed good effect.
> Bombs were dropped on the southern bank of the Humber near East Grimsby upon brightly illuminated factories and sheds which were well hit.
> On their return our airships again were fruitlessly fired at from land and sea and were able to drop their bombs with good effect on the naval forces which were firing at them.

The cutting is marked in ink 24 August 1917 though apparently referring to the raid of 8/9 August the previous year.[75]

HULL: Fifth Zeppelin raid 22 August 1917, L41 Kapitänleutnant Kuno Manger; no bombs on Hull but at Hedon the Primitive Methodist chapel was wrecked, and Roman Catholic chapel, 11 cottages in Baxtergate, and a YMCA hut damaged. (There was an abortive raid on Saturday 2 September 1917. No bombs; no casualties).

HULL: Sixth Zeppelin raid L41 Hauptmann Kuno Manger, Monday and Tuesday, 24/25 September 1917
No deaths.

Typewritten page pinned to back pages of Margaret Strickland-Constable's diary:
> **21/8/17 The Brigade-major of the new staff came after dinner to break it to us gently that the Zepps were expected. He seemed to expect us to be alarmed, but was relieved when we said 'oh, only Zepps'. At 12.50 firing began, and we could see shells bursting and the flashes of bombs falling. I went out into the garden and sat watching it with staff for 3 quarters of an hour. The centre of activity was exactly behind the macrocarpa,[76] and it turned out to have been Hedon. The bombs made very much more noise and much brighter flashes than on the first occasion when we watched them falling upon Hull in 1915. A Methodist chapel and a pigstye were the only buildings damaged, and one old man injured.**
> **By a mistake in the local post office the wrong code word was sent to Capt. Bethell, the one calling out the Volunteers, not the preliminary warning, so he motored all the way to Bridlington, calling out the Volunteers on the way; they all mustered very well and quickly.**
> **One of the sea-planes stationed on the Mere has made a bad landing at Scarborough, and been broken in half; the man was not killed. 'Nothing was left but the floats'. Gen. Clifford said.**
> **Heavy firing was heard at sea about 7a.m. on Aug.28th.**

> **24/9/17 At 10 p.m. that bird of ill omen, the Brigade-major - appeared in the dining-room, and told us that they had just had 'Field-Marshals warnings'. At 10.50**

they had the next warning, and about 1 a.m. Zepps could be heard in the direction of Hornsea. They wandered about for more than an hour, and one went off up the Humber, and one towards Flambro. At 2.45 a.m. we heard bombs, and the raider seemed to dash round, from the Beverley direction, passing over Hull and Hedon, dropping bombs all the way. The bombs were very loud indeed and made a great flash, and our guns were silent and the searchlights almost useless in the fog. The only real damage done was to some small houses in Lansdowne Rd. Hull, and even these still had their roofs on, though rather battered. None killed.

This was the last raid on Hull resulting in physical damage; there were three unconfirmed casualties.

HULL: Seventh Zeppelin raid L63 Kapitanleutnant Michael von Freudenreich, Tuesday 12 March 1918.

Hull Coroner's Inquest 13 March:

1. 7687 **Sarah Masterman** 58, 9 Humber Avenue, Scarborough street, wife of Frank Masterman (core maker), died 12 March, Pickering Park; taken ill after hearing the warning buzzer, near the park, *Hull Daily Mail* 13 March 1918; Dixon p.118.) *Hypertrophy of heart, acute bronchitis. Syncope. Accelerated by shock of a German Zeppelin air raid.*

Bernard Heald recalled this raid:
> After perhaps one hour, we heard gunfire, and this was the signal to tumble out of bed and go downstairs. Mother lit a candle, and as the sound of anti-aircraft gunfire got rapidly louder, we all crouched under the big living room table. Just then we heard a rushing sound rather like the approach of a hissing express train, and then increased in intensity until there was a thud, the ground shook, and the candle jumped off the floor and settled again.

The next day:
> The rushing sound was the noise of a big aerial torpedo being dropped by the raider, the first of the kind to be experienced in the Hull area[77]. It had fortunately landed on agricultural ground where now the Bilton Grange Estate stands, then of course still undeveloped. At the first available opportunity I went to have a look at the crater, and was astonished at its size. It would easily have held two tramcars, and was a big hole, even by later 1939-45 standards.[78]

Margaret Strickland- Constable records what she saw from Wassand Hall, Hornsea :
> 12/3/18
> **WASSAND. At 8.30 Robert and I put on our boots and fur coats and sat down on the terrace to await events. At once we heard the Zepp. droning up the Humber, and presently both Hedon and Hull seemed to be having a terrific bombardment, which we watched for perhaps ½ an hour. Then the Zepp. Came back over Hornsea, and the lake [Hornsea Mere] was most beautifully lighted up by the guns, bombs and searchlights.**
> **After 10 there was a tremendous fresh outburst of firing and bombing, some of the bombs falling in Hornsea, and making quite an alarming noise- began to think about shrapnel, and took R. into the library, where we could watch from the window, and brought Hilary down, but she was very much disgusted because nothing more happened, and she never heard any of the bombs. There was another**

barrage towards12p.m.but no one was hurt, except a woman who died of fright in Hull.
13/3/18
The extraordinary noise that was heard just before the bomb fell are caused by an 'aerial torpedo' but the airman at Brooklands[79] explained that the propeller of the so-called torpedo is only a safety catch.[80]

General Ferrier the officer commanding the Humber garrison retired and was replaced in December 1916 by General Sir Stanley Brenton von Donop, former Master General of Ordnance, and himself of German stock though he never tried to hide this. Unlike many others of German extraction he did not change his name. Von Donop helped establish the local coordinated response to the attackers, involving the anti-aircraft batteries on the coast and along the Humber, and guns sited in Hull. In addition aircraft located at various airfields across Yorkshire, including Beverley, and Hornsea, were sent up to pursue the airships, their machine guns now furnished with explosive and incendiary bullets.

The country was divided into 'warning districts' each some 30-35 miles square. As soon as a raider was within 15-20 miles of the district boundary the controller would telephone all the appropriate persons to initiate action.

An account of the mechanism of interception was recently published by Paul Gannon and is repeated here:

A Tele-net of integrated interception, code-breaking, telecommunications and the direction of defensive forces were at the core of the strategic response devised by the British authorities to a new enemy offensive-Germany's use of airships and long range bombers to raid inland targets.

Airship raids were usually preceded by special weather forecast transmissions, [thus] alerting the British defences. Once the aircraft were underway they sent messages back to their base stating that they were airborne. They also transmitted signals to be used by the German military's own direction-finding network, so that the Zeppelin pilots, say, could be informed where they were located. The German direction-finding triangulation network was confined to a narrower latitudinal zone (from the German border with Denmark to southern Belgium between 51 and 55 degrees north) than the more extensive British network (from southern England to northern Scotland between 49 and 57 degrees north). The British were able to get a more accurate location than the pilots could get from their own bases.

The British direction-finding stations and wireless intercept stations, picking up chatter between attacking airships and their bases, were linked to the War Office in London by direct, dedicated telegraphic lines. At the War Office, Pneumatic Tube Transport systems were used to send incoming direction-finding data direct to a plotting room. This allowed plots of incoming enemy aircraft to be marked within 90 seconds of a direction-finding transmission. Intercepted coded messages went to a special code-breaking unit at the War Office, with its decoded data then sent to the plotting room: here senior officers could advise home defence zones to expect raids to pass overhead at a certain time, enabling night-fighter aircraft to be despatched aloft, and for anti-aircraft batteries to be readied. The combined efforts toward a homeland defence system based around interoperating communications networks was not perfect -----[but] a telling instance

19a. 50 Kilo Zeppelin bomb (Hull Museums).

19b. An array of Zeppelin bombs photographed by Charles Turner; a 300 kilo bomb in the centre, flanked by 100 kilo and 50 kilo bombs (Hull Museums).

19c.Incendiary bomb; Moyses Hall Museum, Bury St. Edmunds.

of how a Tele-net was devised that, without the imperatives of war in the air, might not have come about for years.[81]

The appropriate airfields were informed of the progress of the Zeppelins, their position usually plotted on a grid as reports came in. As they neared the potential target areas visual sightings could not be guaranteed, owing to cloud, poor weather, or the height of the airship. When a squadron received an 'airbandit'[82] call the lack of radar or any means of precisely fixing the altitude and direction of the enemy meant that aircraft were being sent up largely blind, and with little chance of making contact with the enemy.[83]

Defences did however become more effective, with greater numbers of guns and aircraft, which caused the airships to fly higher and higher to avoid damage or destruction. The north of England was however always seriously short of the faster and more modern aircraft capable of climbing with sufficient rapidity to make interception a realistic possibility.

A new breed of Zeppelin was developed, 'the height climber' with a lighter construction and stripped of defensive armament. This meant that it was harder and harder for the airships to find a substantive target on the ground, and latterly the most effective raids were those on London. Its massive urban sprawl and the huge system of docks meant that a significant destructive impact was almost inevitable, however high the airships were forced to fly.

HULL: Eighth Zeppelin raid L56 Kapitanleutnant Walter Zaeschmar, or L63 Kptlt M. Von Freudenreich,

Monday 5/6 August 1918.

No casualties-only a smoke bomb dropped.[84] This was clearly a token attack and an admission the war was over.

These two airships were part of a force of five Zeppelins that had left north Germany with Birmingham probably the main objective. They were in the vicinity of Yarmouth at about 9pm and aircraft took off from the aerodrome quickly locating L70, L65 and L53, but L56 and L63 were some 40 miles away and not observed. Major Egbert Cadbury and Captain Leckie managed to blow a large hole in the fabric of L70 which caught fire and plunged into the sea.[85]

From the eight attacks on Hull the total number of deaths related to air attack confirmed by the coroner's inquests is 55, though the fate of several others was affected by the raids. Most of the casualties were from the first four raids, there were no deaths or injuries in the last one in 1918. One death occurred in the seventh raid, the victim who was already in ill-health died of shock. In 1918-1919 Brooklands Hospital, the officer's hospital at Cottingham, was receiving numbers of victims of influenza, known as the 'Spanish flu', a pandemic which was to kill millions across the globe.[86] On 25 February 1919 the Strickland-Constables were at Sledmere attending the funeral of Sir Mark Sykes M.P. who had been struck down by the disease while at the Versailles peace conference.[87] The allies were discussing the Treaty which would decide the conditions to be imposed on post-war Germany and the reparations that would have to be paid.

A single bomb survives from these attacks, the body and cylindrical tail painted green with the rods, fastening the tail and carcase together, and the nose cone in red. The brass plaque fixed to it is inscribed '50 KILO H.E. BOMB DROPPED FROM A ZEPPELIN ON HULL DURING THE NIGHT OF SEP. 24-25 1917 RECOVERED & EMPTIED BY CAPT. W.R.S.LADELL A.O.D.I.O.O.N.C. (fig.19a,b,c)[88]

Special Constables

There is little in the Hull archives relating to the activities of the Special Constables other than the complete set of the *Special Constables Gazette.* The men were generally over 40, and not younger unless unfit for active service in the armed force or needed for vital service at home. Many of the regular policemen had joined the services leaving the force depleted and with aging personnel. The specials provided essential support in enforcing the blackout,[89] helping to rescue people during air raids, direct them to safety, and giving support to the fire brigade and the medical staff at the various 'dressing stations'. They manned 'motor halts', on every main raid controlling the movement of vehicles and pedestrians through these road blocks after an alarm had sounded. They were also used in the checking of foreign seamen entering the port.

Hull was divided into six districts each under a Special Constable Commander, who was chairman of his local Emergency Committee, of which six subordinates, the Group Leaders, were also members. The latter were allocated two to each of three sub-committees, along with additional members who were designated Sub-Group Leaders. Each sub-group consisted of any number of sections, depending on the total work load and manpower required to undertake particular tasks, each in charge of a Section Leader. There was a Central Organising Committee made up of SCCs and other officials, under the leadership of Chief Special Constable Commander, James Downs J.P. In overall charge was the city's Chief Constable George Morley, appointed in 1910 and in office for the next twelve years. He also was in control of the fire brigade.

First aid posts, referred to as 'Dressing stations' were set up, each headed by a qualified doctor and manned by personnel of the St. John Ambulance association. Boy Scouts and Special Constables acted as telephone attendants and messengers for the stations, Scouts also acted as guides for the old and infirm in the darkened streets. One or two motor vehicles were allocated to each station to enable the injured to be rushed to hospital or transfer medical staff if urgently needed elsewhere. A detachment of Specials was employed as Cyclist Despatch Riders. After an air-raid warning and the lights out order barricades were set up on each of the main roads of the city. At each of these 'motor halts' there was a hut with telephone communication, and all vehicles were stopped except those occupied by known individuals on official business.[90]

The first despatch riders were 40 schoolboys from the Hymers College O.T.C. and when a warning was received, whether or not the buzzers were sounded, set off on their cycles to call out individual special constables from their houses. They were responsible for all of the Central Division and part of the North West. Soon boys from schools across the city, including Scouts and Sea Scouts were on duty throughout the city. Because of the blackout they were allowed to have a light on their cycles, which members of the public did not always understand and occasionally they were hauled from their bicycles and roughly handled. Those Hymers despatch riders with motorcycles were attached to the Headquarters.[91]

Material in the Treasure House (the East Yorkshire county archive) in Beverley fills some of the gaps in our documentation of the specials. A packet contains the personal papers of John William Wilson, including his warrant card dated 17 May 1915, and signed by Major W.H. Dunlop, Chief Constable of the East Riding. Also an arm band (brassard) made of cotton with a buckle fastening, on which is printed or stencilled SPECIAL CONSTABLE in large letters. A letter S has been inscribed by hand above and probably indicates he was a section leader. There is also a very simple circular metal badge, provided with a pin, just like the badges little boys liked to wear. On

20a. Card confirming John William Wilson, as a Special Constable, 17 May 1915 (Treasure House, Beverley).

20b. Brassard of East Yorkshire special constable J.W. Wilson (Treasure House, Beverley).

20c. Pin-on badge of East Yorkshire special constable, J.W. Wilson (Treasure House, Beverley).

the off-white surface is printed a crown, with the words SPECIAL CONSTABLE, above, and GR 1914 below (figs.20a, b,c,d).[92]

After an appropriate length of service a constable was eligible for the Special Constabulary Long Service Medal, instituted 30 August 1919, and though inscribed with the recipient's name, no date or place name is given.

A privately issued silver 'medal'[93] was produced in 1920 on behalf of the Hull Oil Manufacturing Co. Only one example has been seen and the space left for the recipient's name is blank. On one side is a scene of a Zeppelin held in the searchlights, and in the foreground a mobile anti-aircraft gun in action. On the reverse is the inscription' PRESENTED TO------------ BY HOMCO AS A MARK OF APPRECIATION FOR SERVICES RENDERED ON 5TH APRIL 1916 (and laurel leaves below).[94] The raid was soon over after a vigorous response from the artillery and the medal was given to members of the gunnery crews as a thank you for their efforts on that night (fig.21) hence the prominence in the design of the mobile ack-ack gun. Recipients were members of A Section, 1st Anti-Aircraft Brigade, RGA, and of a searchlight detachment of the London Electrical Engineers, though the belief that the Zeppelin crews were able to pin-point individual factories producing materials of strategic importance was of course a misapprehension:

It was evident that the objective was the well known works of the Hull Manufacturing

21. Medal produced on behalf of the Hull Oil Manufacturing Co. (HOMCO) depicting a mobile ack-ack gun shooting at Zeppelin caught in the searchlights (Hull Museums).

Co. Ltd., engaged in manufacturing large quantities of specially treated castor oil so essential for the proper lubrication of the Allies' aeroplanes. [95]

There was evidently some concern about the rather insubstantial nature of the badge worn by the East Yorkshire specials and a better quality replacement was made available as a memento after the war had ended, for which the men were charged 9d. It was probably the same as regards the Hull specials, and the handsome brass lapel badges were almost certainly produced after the end of hostilities. Circular with the three crowns shield of Hull in the brass centre, lettered KINGSTON- UPON- HULL above, and an enamelled outer ring inscribed, SPECIAL CONSTABLE /1914. The enamel is found in white, red and blue, which either marks differences in rank or perhaps length of service (figs.22a,b).[96]

22 a, b. Brass lapel badges of Hull special constables; made by J.R. Gaunt & Son, London (Hull Museums).

There is a booklet of *Instructions to Special Constables* regarding *Air Raids*[97](fig.23), also leaflets regarding the extinguishing of lights,[98]and special instructions in case of enemy invasion, including a leaflet issued 1 December 1914 to the civil population advising general conduct in such an event.[99]

A typewritten letter marked SECRET & CONFIDENTIAL and signed by Captain Percy Runton,[100]the Special Constable Commander for the South Hunsley Beacon Division, dated 26 May 1917, indicates a real fear of invasion at that time[101]:

> For Group Leaders and Deputy Group Leaders only. In view of secret information received respecting the possibility of an attempted enemy landing on the Coast in the near future, IT IS ESSENTIAL THAT YOUR Division should be in complete working order to cope with such an emergency, as per instructions already in force.
> I would however in sending you this secret communication ask that you will see the following points are kept under your observations.
> (1). The absence of any man in your Command being properly notified to you and a substitute detailed in his place temporarily.
> (2). The sending of despatch riders to my headquarters.

(3). That facilities for obtaining the services of any man required in such emergency are in order- for purposes of labour, assisting Military and Police.

It is very essential to successful working that you kindly examine your machinery quietly, and are in a position at the earliest possible moment to deal with an emergency.

Yours faithfully

26th May, 1917   [signed]   Percy Runton Capt.
S.C. Commander

[Added in ink] To/ A.H. Sanderson Esq.
& K. McTurk Esq.

In instructions to the 'specials' it was emphasised that they were non-combatants and should not take up arms against the enemy. This command was probably in light of the brutal treatment meted out to the civilian 'franc tireurs' who put up a brave defence as the German army forced its way through neutral Belgium.

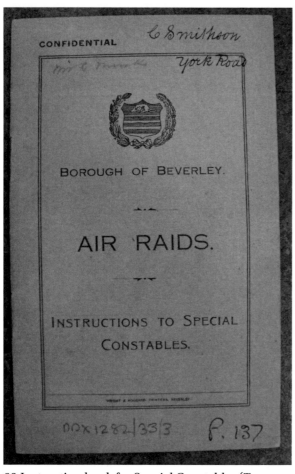

23.Instruction book for Special Constables (Treasure House, Beverley).

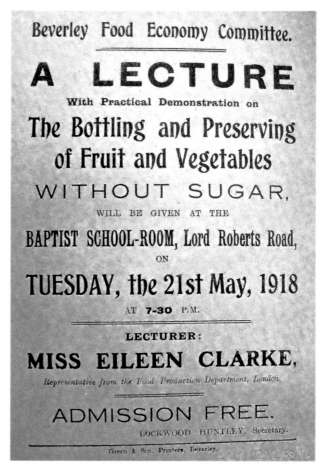

24. Lecture given in Beverley by Eileen Clarke of the Food Production Department, London, 21 May 1918 (Treasure House, Beverley).

The Orderly Boys

An almost forgotten group of young men is the 'Orderly Boys'. Formed in about 1902 by F. W. Bricknell, City Engineer for Hull, to give employment to orphans and boys from families in straitened circumstances.[102] At age 18 they became junior refuse collectors or were placed in various other departments of the council. Organised military fashion as Lance-Corporals, Corporals and Sergeants, each boy was issued with a dress and working uniform, boots, and waterproof cape. Their main role was to keep the streets of Hull clean, the abundant horses then in use providing plenty of work!

There were weekly drills at Londesborough Barracks (Madely Street gymnasium in the winter), and annual camps. Evening pastimes included boxing, football, playing in a band, shooting and swimming. It is likely that like the Scouts they helped to carry messages and were involved in the numerous odd jobs needed to maintain communications between the Specials, the dressing stations and the authorities in general.

The Corn Exchange was their rifle range and in 1912 the Chief Constable received permission from the council for it to be used by members of the police force when not in use by the Orderly Boys.[103] At the outbreak of the 1939-45 war no further boys were recruited, and in 1953 the Trustees were seeking to dispose of their assets.[104]

Cultural activities and the war

War has an impact on all aspects of life including cultural activities, both due to the threat of attack and the fact that artists and performers may have been 'called up.' Equally the potential audience is diminished through individuals having joined the armed services or being fully employed on the 'Home Front.' Membership of the Hull Literary and Philosophical Society dropped from nearly 600 in 1914 to 346 at the end of the war. Despite the dangers of Zeppelin attack a programme of recitals and lectures was maintained, though inevitably the subjects of the latter were war oriented. A war correspondent, a cleric who had been with the Serbian army, and an academic who was with the Russians in Galicia, made their contributions in 1915-16. On 23rd November 1915 the speaker was William Le Queux (1864-1927), journalist and author with a talk entitled 'The German Spy System.'[105] He spent his life warning the world of German militarism and in 1906 published his famous novel of an imagined invasion of Britain, *The invasion of 1910, with a full account of the siege of London*. This best-seller was followed in 1909 by *Spies of the Kaiser* which postulated the existence of a huge network of German agents active throughout the country. In truth there were probably no more than forty spies active pre-war, who were quickly arrested, and attempts by Germany to infiltrate others disguised as neutrals ended in failure, and execution in the Tower of London. Earlier in 1915, following the first Zeppelin raid on Hull 6/7 June there had been attacks on the shops of members of the German community so spies and the possibility of a 'fifth column' were a matter of hot debate.

A Hull citizen Max Schultz, son of an immigrant from Prussia was recruited before the war by the nascent British secret service. His occupation as a yacht broker was excellent cover for visits to Germany to acquire details of vessels being built for the Imperial Navy. Arrested by the police in Hamburg, and tried in Hamburg in November 1911 he was sentenced to seven years imprisonment. Ironically while he was imprisoned in Germany his wife and family back in Hull along with many others with German or foreign names were suffering the anger of the street mobs who threatened their property and personal safety, forcing many to leave the city. Sarah his wife assumed her maiden name of Hilton and when he returned home after the war he too adopted the name of Hilton. He apparently resumed his espionage work for MI6 in Germany but died prematurely 7 September 1924, aged only 49.[106]

The president of the Lit and Phil, 1917-1921, James Downs J.P. was Chief Special Constable Commander, directly answerable to the Chief Constable of Hull. He organised the deployment across the city of Special Constables (all volunteers) whose task was to maintain public order when there was a threat of a Zeppelin attack, enforce black-out, help anyone trying to find their way about the darkened city, and rescue the occupants of bomb damaged buildings. In 1916 Downs also became chairman of Rose, Downs and Thompson, the family engineering firm. He, his brother, and various employees manned battery no.11 of the East Yorkshire Artillery Volunteers.

The museum in Albion street, housed in the building known as the Royal Institution where the Lit and Phil met, remained open to the public. The public display of art in the City Hall was however taken down and placed in the cellars though fearing damage due to the less than perfect storage conditions began to be brought out again in 1916.

Food, war bonds and the sinews of war

There were controls over food distribution in the early part of the war but rationing as understood in the 1939-45 war only began to be introduced rather belatedly in 1917. This was as the result of the German U-boat campaign and the accumulated problems that develop over long periods of warfare when the ever-increasing demands from the front drain the resources at home. Food Economy Committees were established and there were public demonstrations in 'economic cookery', and lectures on 'bottling and preserving of fruit and vegetables without sugar'(fig.24).[107]

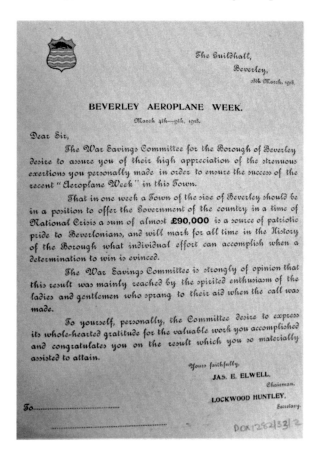

25a. Beverley Aeroplane Week, 4-9 March 1918, which raised £90,000; thank you letter to donors from James Elwell, Chairman, and Lockwood Bentley, Secretary (Treasure House, Beverley).

25b. Beverley War Weapons Week, 15-20th July 1918. Fund raising in the last phase of the war (Treasure House, Beverley).

A 'Beverley aeroplane week', under the chairmanship of James Elwell,[108]had been held 4 -9 March which raised a staggering £90,000, which even now would be regarded as a large sum for a local campaign of limited duration! (figs.25a,)[109]

In July 1918 a 'Beverley War Weapons Week' was held encouraging the public to buy war bonds, with the slogan 'At this serious crisis of THE WAR it is the last determined quarter of an hour that wins'. People were exhorted not to hang on to their 'Bradburys, ie. one pound and ten shilling bank notes, so-called after John Bradbury, Secretary to the Treasury, whose signature appeared on them at the time(fig.25b).[110]

Photographs of bomb damage

Only three photographs showing the results of bombs falling on Driffield (see figs.4a, b)[111] have been found and some showing damage in Goole, otherwise all the pictures located by the present writer record the damage done to property in Hull.

The overwhelming proportion of these, including a number of commercial postcard photographs,[112] were taken after the first raid on the city 5-6 June 1915. An important group of photographs in the Hull Museum were taken by Charles Turner of Turner and Drinkwater, portrait photographers, Regent House, Hull. Along with a written report and map showing locations where bombs landed a set of these were sent to London in a bid to persuade the authorities that Hull needed anti-aircraft guns to defend itself.[113]

The other major collection is the remaining fragment of what seems to have have originally been a comprehensive file of photographs taken by the City Engineers department.[114] There are also some mortuary photographs of victims of the bombing.[115]

After the war a tiny picture album, sold for 6d, 'reproduced from views from the *Hull Daily News* and *Hull Weekly News*', entitled *A pictorial record, Hull and the Zeppelins. Scenes of damage sustained in Hull 1915 -1918.*[116] The ten images, in a pull-out strip with images on either side,[117] were taken by a variety of photographers, but only Marcus Barnard[118] (30 Queen street, in the 'Old Town' area) and Robert Thomas Watson (70 Anlaby road) are named, the rest were presumably by staff photographers on the newspapers.[119]

There is a brief summary of dead and injured inside the front cover, the casualties mostly differing from the accepted figures: Hull 6 June, 25 dead and c.100 injured; Goole, 9 August, 16 dead; Scunthorpe 31 January 1916, 4 dead; Hull 5 March 1916, 17 dead, c.60 injured; Hull, 5 April 1916 Zepps driven off; 9 August 1916 9 dead, several injured, 3 September 1916, Zepps driven off, 21 August 1917 mouth of the Humber, 2 dead from shock; Hedon 24 August 1917, no casualties; Hull 24 September 1917 no casualties; and Hull 12 March 1918, no casualties. It omits the final token raid 5/6 August 1918, when only a smoke bomb was dropped.

John Oliver (of Anlaby Park Methodist church) has informed me of a modified version of the hymn 'Now the day is over'[120] which his father William (born 1905) had learned as child during the 1914-18 War:

> Now the day is over, the night is drawing nigh
> Shadows of the searchlight, steal across the sky
> Children ask in whispers, why the dismal gloom
> Parents answer softly, Zepps expected, soon.

There are surprisingly few physical reminders of the Zeppelin raids directly available to the public, the brass siren, used in both World Wars, and the H.E. bomb, both in the Hull Museums, are the most prominent. There is also the small brass plaque in Holy Trinity church recording bomb damage to the stained glass. The only hint of a personal souvenir of the raids across East Yorkshire appears in a book about 'trench art': 'a brooch made from a Zeppelin bomb which had been found at Spurn Point.'[121]

Acknowledgements

I am indebted for their assistance to David Dixon, the staffs of the History Centre and the Treasure House, Beverley; Robin Diaper, Susan Capes and Caroline Rhodes of Hull Museums, as well as Christine Dunn and Pat Penistone of the Goole Local Studies Library.

Appendix I

Registry of services, church of the Transfiguration, Newington [122]

Sunday 18 October 1914 3p.m

Pound Service for Belgian Refugees 16s 5d

June 6 1915

First Zeppelin raid on Hull. Fires in Drypool, Market Place, Porter street , Campbell street, Pease street, Waller street. 24 deaths and injured

19 December 1916

Pound Service for Prisoners of War £6 6s 7d

2 April 1916

A series of Zeppelin alarms, during the preceding week March 31st, 8.50p.m to 4.20 a.m.; April 1st 8 p.m. to 2 a.m.; April 3rd 8 p.m. to 2.45 a.m.; April 4th 8p.m. to 10a.m.; Wednesday April 5th Air raid on Hull 8p.m.-2 a.m. Driven off by our guns, a few bombs dropped-on the outskirts of East Hull. No lives lost.

24 April Easter Tuesday 7.0 p.m. service.

The 'Hooters' sounded at 9.40 whilst the Sunday School teachers were holding a Social & the 'Relief Hooters' did not sound until 4.20 a.m. No 8a.m. Celebration.[123]

11 June

Memorial service for Lord Kitchener[124] (Second Volunteer Battalion E. Yorks Regiment).

8 August 1916

Zeppelin raid on Hull at 1.30 p.m. Damage done in this Parish very slight. Incendiary bombs dropped in De la Pole & Alliance Avenue, on the Recreation field (5) & a large Aerial torpedo by the embankment of H & B Rway.[125] Great damage in Selby street, Walliker street, Granville street & Sandringham.8 deaths & 2 from shock.

2 September

Zeppelin raid on Hull. Passed over 1.15 a.m. Relief Hooter at 3 a.m.

J.A. Colbeck minister

Appendix II

A small pocket book with brief notes of times on duty and occurrences during alarms; kept by Gwyneth Milburn, a V.A.D. nurse on duty during the Zeppelin raids on Hull. This is transcribed from a photocopy sent to the late Chris Ketchell by Col. Gleadow, Ampleforth, in 1989. He was a nephew of Col. Henry Milburn, Gwyneth's father.

Col. Henry Charles Milburn (b.1860-d.1948, aged 88) O.B.E., M.B., B.S. was responsible for establishing 11 auxiliary hospitals for wounded soldiers and 26 dressing stations to care for casualties of the air-raids.

After graduating he was house surgeon at Durham County Hospital for three years before becoming consulting surgeon at the Victoria Children's Hospital in Hull. A major figure in the B.M.A., he was Deputy Commissioner for No.6 District of the St. John Ambulance Brigade 1898-1903. Milburn was at the No.2 British Red Cross Hospital, Rouen, in 1915, and worked on the hospital trains in France and Belgium, returning to England in 1918. Divisional Medical Officer (Ministry of Health) for North East England until 1925. He died in a nursing home at Harrogate in 1948.

June 4th 11p.m. to 2.15 a.m.

June 6th 1915

10- p.m.- Hooters go-Fire station ring up Dad - all lights out-
        get dressed again-get uniform ready & haversacks. Fill baths

10-20 p.m. Mr. Howell just come to [ask] if he is to go on duty at

Rest Station[126]-Dad tried to get Miss Abbott on 'phone, but
could'nt get through.

10-30- Mother and I get into uniform-

10-45- Go to Rest Station with Mr. Howell.

11-45 Explosions all round us-2 fires-
writing in dark 12 striking[127]
5 or 6 bombs- glass shattered

****

12-15 standing by gates- awful fire raging over Whitefriargate
Way - engine driver says

¼ to 1 Miss Abbott Beaver & Marshall
came on duty
Sat in cellar of station- then went to Rest Station

1-10-Left station-Left the others in charge-

2-25 go to bed

3-45 a.m. Officer came to use telephone to order shell [a light, temporary coffin] to be
sent round to Campbell st. for body found among the ruins-

People walking up & down Campbell st. all night-

<u>Monday June 9th 1915</u>

Whole terrace in Campbell st. (opposite us) shattered. A man & his daughter missing- St.
Thomas' Church-nine holes in roof-windows broken-One house the windows are all blown out,
& half the plaster off the ceiling; but some glass ornaments on the mantelpiece not even cracked.
Windows of a house five doors from us, cracked. Also

****

Mrs. Jones kitchen & bedroom windows. House in South Parade burnt-Two children killed whilst
in bed with their mother. Her hair singed –Her husband is in France fighting-

<u>Tuesday- June-8th[sic].1915</u>

10-15- Hooters go-get dressed- Mrs Forty & Ethel come in
to us- Fill baths[128]- Turn gas off and water

11-45 Dismiss

<u>June-15th-1915</u>

9-25 Hooters go   ------- [faint and illegible]--------

1-40 Dismiss

<u>June 21st 1915</u>

11-5 Hooters go-

11-15- Mother ------ me -----sit on chairs on doorstep

2 a.m- Go to bed

?-25-   Dismiss

<u>August-9th -1915</u>

8-40. Hooters go-

9-45- Go to bed

10.30 Dismiss

Zeppelins over Ulrome, South Cave Goole-

<u>August-10th 1915</u>

11-35 –Hooters go-

2-a.m. Private message saying all over

3-45 Special Constables dismissed by cyclists,

with no authority

----30- Dismiss by the hooters-

August- 12th 1915

8-20 p.m. – Alarm

2-30 a.m- Private dismiss-

2-40 a.m-Dismiss by hooters-

Zeppelins over Harwich-6 killed-23 injured

Over Leicester, but no damage done-

August -15th 1915

11-25 p.m. Alarm

11-30- Dad calls me-Mothers away-Fill baths-& jugs-

12-   Call Maggie & Josy-

1-a.m. Dismiss

August-17th 1915

-p.m.   - Alarm

-5- Arrive at Paragon Station, from Beverly [sic]- station in total
   Darkness. Walk up home-Barge into different people

-55   Dismiss

September 8th 1915

Filey - p.m Heard Zeppelins were somewhere on coast-supposed to have
been near Whitby& Eastern Counties-Alarm never went at Hull-

September 9th 1915

Zeppelins again out- Emily's window rattled at a.m.

Alarm in Hull sounded at [-----]

Dismiss at 2.40 a.m.

Damage done at [------]

Hear to-day ( ) one bomb dropped the other side of the Brigg at
same time as the windows

---------------? – 10 p.m.

November 26th 1915

1-55 p.m.   Alarm.   Brian Cracroft left at 11-30 to go round the
      Guards as Garrison Orderly Officer.

February-Thursday 1916

Alarm- 6.10-p.m. Ist Dismiss 7-30

Alarm 7-40 – Dismiss-9 p.m.

Sunday-Feb. 13th 1916

Alarm- 8- Dismiss 9 – At Swanland

March -5th 1916 Sunday

Alarm – 8-30 p.m.   Snow thick by

11 p.m.- Heard engines of Zeppelin at 12-5

Bombs exploded   -   First saw flash in sky & awful noise- Bombs
dropped at intervals till after 1-a.m.. Damage in Bean st., Day St,
   Reports- Hull & East Riding Club[129] damaged-

Mr. Kent's lodgings in Linnaeus St.

> Zeppelin seen for 7 minutes stationary opposite our house-
> Two Zeppelins seen-
> Dismiss- 2-55 a.m.

Appendix III

David Neave has brought my attention to some recollections of the raids in the *Hull Daily Mail* Friday 4 June1965 by the Rev. C.E.B. Cowburn, who from 1928-31 was minister of the Queens road Methodist church, which was destroyed in the 1939-45 war. During that time he was minister at Thornaby-on-Tees. Here he was an air raid warden and helped to organise groups of street fire-fighters and established his Sunday School premises as a rest centre for those displaced by the bombing.

Cowburn's reminiscence of the 1914-18 war are as follows:

The night I was chased by a Zepp.

In 1915 I was a dispatch-rider with the special constables, the only form of volunteer civil defence we had in those early days of the first Great War.

My instructions, in the event of a threatened air attack, were to cycle round calling up fellows members in my area and then to place myself at the disposal of our section leader.

June 6 that year, as in this, fell on a Sunday.

At 10 in the evening the alarm began to sound from Blundell's mill, soon to be taken up by all the 'buzzers' all over the city.

In view of the din 'calling up' became a mere formality as the CALLED AND GONE cards exhibited at the various addresses confirmed. In due course I reported at the rendezvous, which was at the corner of Hessle-road and Walker street. Here a dozen 'specials' had already assembled.

Half an hour went by without incident.

People stood gossiping at their front doors and regarding us with some amusement. It looked like yet another false alarm, and we waited impatiently for the dismissal [ie.'all clear'].

The night was far from dark, for the moon was in her last quarter, but it was pretty boring having to hang about without rhyme or reason.

The real thing

We began to get restless. Soon after 11.30 the commandant drove up visiting rounds. 'No, he said, in replay to our enquiries, 'this is not a false alarm but the real thing. A Zepp was over the city about 11 o'clock, although it dropped no bombs. It was last reported over the city about 11o'clock, although it dropped no bombs. It was last reported across the river, somewhere near Stallingborough. Keep your eyes skinned.' And off he went.

As we stood listening to the sound of the car fading away in the distance, we became aware of another and most peculiar noise.

'What on earth's that? ' asked one man.

'It's Follet's car' said another, 'What else could it be?'[130]

A third suggested it might be a motorboat on the river.

The sound came nearer, more insistent, more powerful than anything produced by a car or motorboat---- a heavy beating sound, for all the world like a gigantic threshing machine.

We stared at each other without speaking.

Then someone exclaimed, 'Whats that over the pier?'

We saw what he meant, a vague amorphous 'something' in the semi-darkness.

Suddenly there came a flash which lit up the entire under structure of 'the thing,' revealing to our startled eyes, the cigar-like shape of an enormous Zeppelin. The flash was succeeded by a terrific detonation.

An enemy airship had dropped the first-ever bomb on Hull.

Then she began to move.

That bomb probably fell on Queen-street, some three-quarters of a mile away and the Zepp was heading northwards, so we were hardly in the target area. But it was obvious policy to get the folk off the streets, so we scattered.

Demoralising

For my part I ran down Walker-street shouting to the excited knots of people to go indoors.

The Zepp held on its course, which I was relieved to note was parallel to mine, and dropping bombs at intervals.

Some of the explosions were quite loud, others not so loud. The latter, as it turned out, were incendiaries, one or more of which set Edwin Davis's store in the Market Place ablaze.

I was scared. The bombing of course, was not to be compared with what we had to endure subsequently in the later war. But it was a novel experience in those days to be attacked from the air.

And after all, bad though it is to be at the mercy of microscopic silvery gnats miles up in the skies, it is truly demoralising to be bombed by a thing the size of an Atlantic liner from 4000 ft or so.

As I pounded down Walker-street I was joined by a soldier and a uniformed policeman, though where they came from I cannot tell.

On we ran together and all the while I kept watching the Zepp out of the tail of my eye. Then to my dismay, I realised it was gradually veering round and heading now in our direction.

'My God', gasped one of my companions, 'She's coming right over us!' With that both of them vanished into a neighbouring house, and I found myself once more running alone.

On either side

I take no credit for not following their example. The fact is, I was quite incapable of swerving aside. I knew one direction only, and that was full speed ahead.

As the Zepp passed overhead two more bombs dropped simultaneously. One fell on the house to one side of me, the other on its opposite number across the way.

Fortunately for the homes concerned (not to speak of myself) these happened to be incendiaries which failed to go off.

But the very next bomb proved to be a high explosive which burst with an almighty crash in a neighbouring street.

With that my nerve went completely. I fairly flew round the corner on to the Anlaby-road desperately seeking cover. A shop entrance offered the only visible refuge so I made for a row of plate glass windows. Scarcely bomb-proof it is true, but I was in no mind to pick and choose.

The first I came upon, Tate and Oglesby's china shop, had its gate drawn across. So had the next. But the entrance to Cusson's was open. In I darted and made myself as small as possible on the floor.

Pathetic sight

Eventually I regained control over myself and emerged from my retreat. It was now midnight. The raider, or raiders, had passed, but there was plenty of noise in the streets. Whistles were blowing, ambulance bells clanging, and, most blood-curdling of all, cries of 'Help!' were coming from one direction in particular.

I made my way towards it and came upon a distressing sight. The high explosive bomb I had heard explode as I ran had shattered a terrace of small hoses in Campbell-street. In one home, pathetically enough, preparations had evidently been made for a wedding reception on the morrow. A smashed-up wedding cake lay among the debris. On the roof below the clerestory window of St. Thomas's Church a mattress (or was it something more tragic?) had been blown by the blast.[131]

So begrimed by dust was it that it was impossible to distinguish exactly what it may have been.

Defenceless

However the regular police and firemen were in charge by this time. I left it to their more capable hands, and somewhat shaken and very, very weary, turned my steps homewards.

It transpired that some 25 people were killed. The city was utterly defenceless, since we had no 'ack-ack' at the time.

True a destroyer moored in one of the docks had loosed off a few rounds, but her guns were unable to achieve the necessary elevation, and her shells probably did more damage to the town than to the enemy.

It was never clearly established whether one, or more than one Zepp was involved. But it was believed that the leader was the celebrated German airship commander Captain Mathy, doomed to perish in a subsequent raid on this country.

Following the publication of the recollections of the Rev. Cowburn two other individuals offered their reminiscences, *Hull Daily Mail*, 9 June 1965.

Fred Rands who until his retirement was a sub-editor of the *Hull and Yorkshire Times*:

On the night of June 6, 1915, I had to walk practically from one end of the city to the other —from Goddard-avenue to East Hull. I was about opposite the Alexandra Theatre when the approaching Zeppelin was first heard- I continued my way over the old North Bridge and had got as far as Holderness Hall before the raider was overhead.

As I scanned the sky I heard two or three men, standing at the corner of Dansom-lane, say, "There he is." I nipped across the road to join them and there could see the Zeppelin in black outline.

A nightmare

It was fairly low and whirring along in a manner that did not seem ominous until a dull thud and a blaze of light on the road opposite the Windmill Hotel told us that the first incendiary bomb had been dropped. In the midst of the flames I noticed a steel rod with a loop handle. I mentally noted it as an interesting souvenir when it had cooled off, but such thoughts were quickly dispelled by what happened in the next few seconds.

Terrific crashes indicated that high explosive bombs had found their mark in the Bright-street area and a timber yard just behind us. These suddenly transformed a tranquil night into a hideous nightmare, and I must confess that the little group I was with scattered quickly.

There were no air-raid shelters to dive into, and I dashed back across the road and ran along Witham, close to the walls of buildings, until I came to Malton-street corner.

Looking upwards, I saw that the raider seemed to be directly overhead and, in my excitement, I galloped through several little streets until I emerged into East-street This was no wider than the width of a lorry and, as I neared its end I found myself against a little cottage on the left-hand side. Some strange impulse caused me to shoot straight across the road at right angles.

As I landed on the opposite pavement there was another terrific crash and I was flung full length to the ground, shaken and bruised, I careered along Clarence-street to the accompaniment of more heavy explosions and the insistent loud whirring of Zepp engines. As I fled along Great Union-street, the ordeal became more tense as shots came from HMS Adventurer lying in Earle's yard. By the time I found myself at North Bridge again, I was thoroughly winded and feeling deadly sick.

Grim moment

The Zepp was humming aloft and appeared to be making towards Wincolmlee. I gaped at it with the thought that he was going to make some big fires among the oil mills. If that had been the raider's purpose, he could not have gone wrong, but he held his hand and the huge vessel swung round in half a circle and passed over the Old Dock Bridge in Lowgate, to the Market-place. There Edwin Davis's building met its fate and Holy Trinity Church had a miraculous escape.

I turned homewards once more and had walked from North Bridge to St. Andrew's Church when the Zepp came wafting back in almost complete silence from Stoneferry way. After my previous experience, I was not in the mood for a lot more running and in fact, had come to the conclusion, that it was not worth while.

I decided to get out of the way of possible danger from falling masonry by hopping down Abbey-street to the side of the wooden railway fence right opposite Southcoates Station. Meanwhile the Zeppelin had halted its flight and with engines stopped, it hung low in the air in sinister silence.

This was broken with grim and tragic results as I saw the two bombs launched from the gondola which fell on the terrace in Waller street with devastating effects to life, limb and property.

No sleep

There was no sleep in East Hull that night, and, traversing Clarence -street once more in the morning, I stood aghast at the sight which the corner of East -street presented. The little cottage had been shattered and an aged couple killed in their bed; yet amidst all this wreckage a picture of Queen Victoria was still hanging on the wall undisturbed. The moral of my story is the folly of getting into a panic. All my wild running only took me into more danger, and if I had stood still at the onset I might have got my little souvenir from the road near the Windmill Hotel.

Harold Wright, overseer of the *Hull Daily Mail* composing room, provides the following. He retired soon after it was published:

I was 15 when the first Zeppelin raid occurred. We lived in Egton-street and when the siren sounded, people got up.

I went into the timber yard in Dansom Lane, about 300 yards from where the first bomb fell. Then I remembered that everyone had been told to stay inside if the Zeppelins came. The bomb brought me to my senses.

The part which I recall most clearly is from the raid itself is making for shelter and shouting to other people, 'Get in! Get in!'

Nobody took any notice.

But perhaps my most vivid recollections of the affair as a whole is an incident on the night after the raid.

It had created a great deal of anger and tension and on the Monday evening in Cleveland- street, the police were out to control the crowds.

Officers had pushed them back to Jennings-street and Hodgson-street, and seemed to have everything under control.

Then a bare-headed old lady wearing an apron was allowed through, she walked calmly along the street. Nobody was taking any notice of her. Then, suddenly she pulled a flat iron from under her apron and flung it through the window of a German pork butcher's shop.

Blaze of fury

Immediately, this set the crowd alight. They broke through, knocking the police aside, and all made for the shop. People were running down side streets carrying meat, and I saw a piano hurled from a bedroom window above the shop.

This was only one of several attacks on German shops. There were others in Porter-street and Holderness-road, and people even went to a German's house on Holderness High-road to smash the windows.

There was an ironical touch about the first raid. A number of Hull people who had heard of bombs being dropped at Goole on the previous Friday cycled there on Saturday morning to see the damage.

If they had waited a day, they could have saved themselves the journey.

Appendix IV

Four diaries written by Stanley Duncan (1878-1954) are preserved at the BASC (British Association for Shooting and Conservation) headquarters: book 2, 1911-16, and book 3, 1916-25 contain references to the Zeppelins over Hull and the Humber. A railway engineer with the North Eastern Railway, he was founder in 1908 of the Wildfowlers Association of Great Britain and Ireland (WAGBI), now the British Association for Shooting and Conservation. Author with Guy Thorne of the *Complete Wildfowler-Ashore and Afloat*, 1911; revised and reprinted, 1950. He established a gun shop in Hull continued by his sons. Initially on the Anlaby road, latterly in Paragon Square, and currently on the Willerby road, the firm is no longer linked to the Duncan family.

Stanley Duncan, a keen wildfowler, hated to let a day slip by without him going down to the Humber shore to try his luck. He inserts references to the war and the Zeppelin raids in his pocket shooting diaries. Some are labelled 'MEMO BOOK North Eastern Railway'. The entries are brief, recording the birds shot and the names of those who accompanied him. The earliest reference to hostilities is 25 August 1914:

We shot on the 25th until after 9-0 p.m. Heard about this hour a violent report – many miles from us but very loud. Never heard its equal before. War raging – gun boats (two off Grimsby) no interference with shooting on this shore.
21 September 1914: *T. W. leaving on 22nd by car. He had seen a hydroplane [ie. a seaplane] drop a practice bomb off Grimsby.*

A fortnight later, 5 September, he records the ominous news:

Shooting Prohibited due to the War. Notice by the police, signed Major Dunlop.
  There seems to have been an accommodation with the authorities for he and other shooters carried on, taking a bag which included rabbits and partridges.
  On 6 March 1916 at 12.05 a.m.:
  Zepps over Hull until 1.20 a.m. Second Raid. Saw Zeps on both occasions 'Frightful Machines'. Height probably 3 miles. Saw bombs drop. All the people terrified. 2 in. of snow on the ground, slight N. wind & before sunrise [an]other 2in. snow fell. Damage considerable.

5 April 1916: 9.00 p.m. Zepps – one on fringes of town – said to be another coming in on Lincs. side. Driven off splendidly by 8 or 9 search lights & hot gun fire. No one killed. Four bombs dropped on outskirt.

27 November 1916: Zepps over N. E. Coast. Two brought down in the N. Sea. Bravo. One off Durham coast the other off Norfolk.

14 March 1917: By an order of the Board of Agriculture & Fisheries – made 14th inst. Wildfowling shooting permitted till end of March-Birds may be sold until April 15th.

21 August 1917: Patrington. Zepp raid. Dropped bombs on Hedon. Kept out of gun ranges in attempting to reach Hull. Many shots were fired at it but she was 'out of shot.' I saw her in the lights. She was very high. Probably four miles. Home 3.0 a.m. into Paragon [station].

5 August 1918: (Bank Holiday) Air Raid alarm at night. One Zepp for certain brought down [not so].

11 November 1918: Date of Armistice Great European War.

The diaries thereafter continue solely with record of birds taken and names of some of his shooting companions.

Appendix V

Mrs Elizabeth Andrew for 21 years in charge of the telephone exchange at Ferriby (nr. Hull), located in her house. On her 80th birthday was the subject of a piece in the Mount Benger (New Zealand) newspaper, 15 September 1920:

> Until a month or five weeks ago I had to attend to all calls after 8.30 at night. I never could go to bed till 11.30 and then I often had to come downstairs and attend to calls. It was very bad when the military were here, and worst of all on Zeppelin alarm nights. There was no bed for me then.
>
> One week there were alarms every night, and I never got to bed till 5 o'clock in the morning. I had to remain at the switchboard.
>
> Sundays were also a botheration. I have been on duty as long as 16 hours on a stretch.[132]

Recent publications

Harry F. Baxter *The Soldier and the Orderly Boys* Bedford 1999.

Arthur G. Credland *The Hull Zeppelin Raids 1915-1918* Fonthill, 2014 (this gives details of the earlier source material).

Thomas Fegan *The Baby Killers-German Air Raids on Britain in the First World War* Barnsley, 2002, 2012.

Jon Guttman *Zeppelin vs British Home Defence 1915-1918* Oxford, 2018.

Gareth Jenkins *Zeppelins over Bury -the raids on Bury St. Edmunds* Needham Market, revised edition 2016.

John Markham *Keep the Home Fires Burning* Beverley 1988.

Susanna O'Neill *Great War Britain-Hull and the Humber, Remembering 1914-18* Stroud, 2015.

Nigel J. Parker *Gott Strafe England-the German Air Assault against Britain 1914-1918* Helion 2015. Ditto Vol.2, 2016.

Ditto Vol.3, 2019.

Peter J.C. Smith *Zeppelins over Lancashire-the story of the air raids on the county of Lancashire in 1916 and 1918*, 1991

Zeppelin and airship memorabilia

Auction catalogues of the David Kirsch Collection of Zeppelin and other airship memorabilia:

Pt.1, 21 March 2012 *Wallis and Wallis* Lewes, East Sussex

Pt.2, 25 July 2012

Pt.3, 28 November 2012
Pt.4, 12 June 2013.

Notes

1   Arthur G. Credland *The Hull Zeppelin Raids 1915-1918* Fonthill, London, 2014.
2   Thirteen in some sources.
3   Buzzer or siren were the usual names given to air-raid warning whistles in the Second World War,
4   These were the same sort of whistles, used by manufacturers to mark the beginning and ending of the working day, and usually referred to as 'factory hooters'. Those that marked the working day at the Metal Box factory in Gipsyville were certainly still called hooters in the 1950s.
5   Street illumination was gas-light, and town houses were almost universally gas too, though in the country oil lamps and candles were still common.
6   The current *Hull Daily Mail* building is on the site.
7   Hull Museums; Acc. No. 2012.132. Cast into the piping at the base of the steam whistle is the founders name, though some of the raised letters have been lost:on one side ALEX—NDER/REG N° and on the opposite side G C---S/HULL/--TD. Overall length 55 in(140.1cm) main cylinder 40in(101.cm)and girth 28.5in(72.4cm).
8   John Buchan *Mr. Standfast* 1918.
9   *Yorkshire Post* Saturday 21 December,1919, p.9, col.1.
10   Which was not unusual unless there was a clear view of the ground, and of recognisable features. There was no radar or other means of penetrating cloud and mist.
11   The writer presumably means searching for a path to a major target.
12   Treasure House, DDBG/214/1.
13   Born Margaret Elizabeth Pakenham she married, in 1898, Frederick Strickland Constable heir to Wassand Hall near Hornsea. See DDST/1/8/2/1-3, covers 1915-1917.
14   J.R.R. Tolkien convalesced at Brooklands in 1917-18, recovering from trench fever contracted at the Somme.
15   The Bethell family of Rise Hall (contemporary sources refer to Rise Park), E. Yorks.
16   Margaret Strickland-Constable's daughter.
17   One of Mrs. Strickland-Constable's children.
18   Continuing the account in the issue for 21 December 1919.
19   Wine and Spirit merchants, 69 High street.
20   Steam Ship Agents, Forwarding Agents and Warehouse Keepers, 71 High street, and also Maritime Buildings, Alfred Gelder street.
21   *Yorkshire Post* 21 December 1919, p.9, cols. 1 and 2.
22   Ibid, col.2. A description of the second raid on Tyneside follows this; fourteen were killed at Jarrow, two others later dying in hospital. A police constable was killed at Willington Quay.
23   Treasure House, Beverley DDBB/2/4/2.
24   Her husband.
25   There was a constant fear of spies and a 'fifth column'. None of the scares were ever substantiated.
26   Presumably a family pet.
27   See below; the conclusions of all the relevant inquests are listed, 25 in all. The newspaper report of an unidentified body recovered from the ruins of Edwin Davis seems to be misreporting. There is no mention of an unknown woman, killed in the raid, to be found in the volume of inquests, though unidentified bodies found on the streets or pulled from the docks etc are all recorded.
28   Argyle street, off the Anlaby road and not far from the railway station, an obvious target.
29   Lord Lieutenant of East Yorkshire.
30   Inquisition Book NC/1/1/4/9; the Treasure House, Beverley. The numbered entries are taken from the record of coroner's inquests at Hull. The descriptions in italics of the cause of death are from this source but the entries here are filled out with further details provided by the newspapers and the work done by Dixon on the burial records from the cemeteries in west and east Hull. There are occasional discrepancies of age and date of death, those recorded by the coroner have been used as probably the most reliable. P.M. indicates a post mortem examination.
31   The conclusions of each inquest is recorded in the 'inquisitions' book; each individual given a unique number.
32   David Dixon *Kingston upon Hull, World War I airship raids 1915-18. The names and burial details for the known people who died,* privately published, 2014(revised edition),18pp.
33   Treasure House, Beverley, NC/1/1/4/9.
34   Coroner's inquest 26 March 1915 following a post mortem; Treasure House, Beverley NC/1/1/4/9.
35   *Yorkshire Post* 21 December, p.9, col.2.
36   Using the intelligence reports at the National Archives identifies the captain of the L 11 as Oberleutnant Freiher von Buttlar. See Nigel J. *Parker Gott Strafe England: the German air assault against Great Britain 1914-18* vol.1, Helion,2015, pp.173-4..

37   T. Bernard Heald *Times winged chariot* Hutton Press 1985, pp.98-9.

38   Parker, vol.1,p.196,again identifies the captain of L11 ,from the intelligence reports.

39   A photograph exists of the Courtney Street Volunteer Night Patrol of 1915; see Credland 2014, illustration 25.

40   Syd Smith was a tobacconist at this address and the production of the postcard was evidently a private venture; Hull Museums; Acc.no.2006.10514. It is addressed to 'Miss I. Wear 201 Walton street Anlaby road' but appears not to have been posted. In 1915 Edward Hyde Wear is recorded as a postman at this address.

41   Henry Miles, printer, 76 Charles street; Hull Museums; Acc. No.1986. 421. Doggerel verse was produced in some abundance and published in newspapers, magazines and on postcards.

42   George Thorp diaries, vol.9, January-June,1916,37v (Hull History Centre).

43   Hull Museums; Acc.no. 578.1986).

44   General Officer commanding of the Humber Garrison.

45   Thomas Fegan *The 'Baby Killers'* Barnsley, 2002.

46   Sixteen is the usually accepted number of dead.

47   *Yorkshire Post* 21 December, p.9. cols. 1 and 2.

48   Shuffelton, a district of Goole on the Hook road.

49   Major German port with which Goole and Hull had major trading links during peacetime.

50   Reference to the imperial German idea of 'culture', emphasising its own superiority, subordination of the individual to the state, and a demand for practical efficiency.

51   In the East Yorkshire vernacular this would have been 'bains' rather than the bairns of Scotland and the north-east of England.

52   Joseph Compton Rickett, Liberal M.P., later an M.P. at Pontefract, and Paymaster General, 1916-19.

53   Local Studies, Goole Library.

54   Susan Butler *Goole a pictorial history* vol. 2.

55   Evelyn Laye *Boo to my friends* 1958.

56   *Goole Times* 13 August 1915, p.4.

57   *Goole Times* 20 December 1918; and contemporary sources.

58   Butler, see above.

59   There were no defences when L21 raided York 2 May 1916; there were nine civilian deaths and one soldier was killed. Guns and searchlights were in place for the second raid (25 September 1916) by L14, and damage was limited though a woman died of shock. A third and last attack 27/28 November, by L13, caused little damage, most of the bombs were dropped on Barmby Moor. See Thomas Fegan *The 'Baby Killers' German air-raids on Britain in the First World War* Barnsley 2002.

60   Thomas Fegan *The 'Baby Killers'* Barnsley, 2002.

61   The German General Staff decided in September 1914 that all airships should be used 'at the dark of the moon', ie. in the period some eight days before and after the new moon. This meant they were a less conspicuous target but made accurate navigation more difficult; without modern aids like radar a visual sighting was essential to identify the target. Frequently it was only from information gathered after the raid that the airship crews knew exactly where they had been.

62   Ie. in the 1939-45 war.

63   P.C. Sands, C.M. Haworth, and J.H. Eggleshaw *A history of Pocklington School, East Yorkshire,1514-1980* Highgate Publications,Beverley,1988.

64   Donald Dallas *James Purdey & Sons ,gun and rifle makers, two hundred years of excellence* London 2013,pp.249-250.

65   To his wife from 9 Buckingham Gate, SW,3 August 1916; Hull History Centre, UDDSY2/1/2F/59.

66   Like Goodwood race course.

67   This is exactly what happened to L48 which came to earth at Theberton, Suffolk, 17 June 1917.See photograph in Thomas Fegan *The 'Baby Killers'* 2nd edition 2012 ,p.172.

68   The Cairo museum of antiquities.

69   Paul Cambon (1843-1924) French diplomat at the embassy in London. He helped negotiate the Entente Cordiale in 1904 and was the French signatory to the Sykes-Picot agreement (see note 87).

70   Harold Nicolson and Vita Sackville West. Nicolson worked at the Foreign Office and both men were present at the peace talks in Paris after the war.

71   Letter terminates in short signature or quotation in (ancient?) Greek. It was addressed to his wife but the words, where one would expect 'Dear----', are unintelligible; Hull History Centre DDSY2/1/2F/59.

72   Pyott was awarded the DS.O.

73   Sir Charles Wakefield, (1859-1941) founder of Castrol, the lubricants company. Later he became Baron Wakefield, and then Viscount Wakefield.

74   He also contributed a cartoon to the *Special Constables Gazette*; see Credland 2014.

75   Hull History Centre, a newspaper cutting, 24 August 1917, LDBHR/1/4/4.

76   A cypress tree.

77   Such devices were reported from the sixth raid on Hull 24 September 1917; see Credland 2014, p.79.

78 Heald, p127.

79 The officers' hospital at Cottingham;seeabove.

80 Treasure House, Beverley DDST/1/8/2/3.

81 Paul Gannon *E & A*,16 June 2014.

82 The contemporary expression. In WW2 enemy aircraft were referred to simply as 'bandits' and plotted with the appropriate 'angel' number, indicating height ie. angels 15 (rendered as one, five) would be 15,000 feet.

83 Land based aircraft at Beverley Westwood, various stations in Lincolnshire, as well as the West Riding provided air cover for East Yorkshire. The Royal Naval Air Service established a station at Lillingholme (Lincs.) in July 1914 which operated mainly floatplanes in cooperation with the former Humber ferry , the paddle-steamer *Killingholme*. A sub-station was opened at Hornsea Mere in July 1915, operating the Sopwith Baby (built by Blackburns at their Leeds factory) and the Short 184; see Geoff Simmons 'Then and now-a study into the military aerodromes and landing grounds of the 1914-18 war in the East Riding of Yorkshire', pt.3 Royal Naval Air Service, Hornsea Mere', *East Yorkshire Historian* ,vol.2, 2001,pp.80-6.

84 *Hull Times* 29 January 1919.

85 Nigel J. Parker *Gott Strafe England* vol.2.pp.380-388.

86 Margaret Strickland-Constable ; Treasure House, Beverley DDST/1/8/3.

87 Sir Mark Sykes (1879-1919), Lt. Colonel in the Green Howards, elected as M.P. for Hull Central in 1912 and succeeded as 6th baronet in 1913. Served in the Boer War and became a specialist in Middle-Eastern affairs, being the co-author of the Sykes-Picot agreement which set out the English and French spheres of influence within the Middle East to be assigned after the defeat of the Ottoman Turks (see note 69).

88 Hull Museums; Acc. No. 2011.223. Length overall 41in (104.2cm), cylinder tail 9 7/8in diameter(225cm). Carcase of bomb 27in(68.5cm), maximum girth 36 in(91.4cm).The rods joining tail piece with carcase each 26 ¼ in (67.1cm), and 7in (18.2cm)across from outside of one rod to outside edge of its pair.

89 Treasure House, Beverley, DDX/282/48/28.

90 See Credland 2014, especially chapter 4 and accompanying notes.

91 See *Hull and East Yorkshire Times* (*Hull Times*)1 February 1919,col.8.p.3.This was the second of three Zeppelin Memorial issues, see also 25 January and 8 February.

92 Treasure House, Beverley, DDMT/613.

93 The example described has no means of suspension.

94 Hull Museums ; acc.no.2007.5903. Birmingham hall mark,1920-1 and makers initials WJD.

95 *Hull Museum Publications* vol.140, pp. 23-4. The recipients were: H. Ivan Hardy, W.F. Dowse, F.S. Hunt, H. Rood, A.E. Buckland, C.G. Wiggins, R. Keen, C. Floyd , E. Lansdell, J. Didymus, H.J. Honey, A. Johnson, C.J. Archard, L. Goodinson, H.W. Dixon, R. Todd, A.K. Green, H.P. Waterhouse, H. Linsdell, E.P. Pearce(father of),A.G. Bilton, E.T. Chisnell, A.T. Wootton, and H.E. Chastney.

96 Of the three examples in the Hull Museum, two have crescent shaped flanges for insertion in a lapel button hole, and the third a hinged pin fastening. This later is stamped on the back of the badge J.R.GAUNT LONDON, also stamped on one of the lapel flanges. Accession numbers 57.63.2, 389.1987 and 57.63.1, left to right in illustration.

97 Treasure House, Beverley, DDX1282/33/3.

98 Ibid. DDX1282/48/28.

99 Treasure House , Beverley, DDBB/2/1//4.

100 Percy T. Runton, architect and surveyor, White House, Davenport Avenue, Hessle. Partner in the firm of Runton and Barry, commissioned to build, starting 1908, the Hull Garden Village for employees of Messrs Reckitts, manufacturers of household products, such as black lead, starch, and Dettol (now Reckitts-Benckeiser, or RB). Runton and Barry also built as a speculative venture of their own, starting 1912, the Garden Village on the western outskirts of Hull, known as Anlaby Park.

101 Treasure House, Beverley, DDMT/613.

102 The most extensive account of this body of young men is Harry F. Baxter *The soldier and the Orderly Boys* 1999, though he was under the impression they were formed towards the end of the Great War.

103 Hull City Council Minutes , Property Committee, 1912,p.113.

104 Hull History Centre, Memo 1953, T MK/1/5/24.

105 Margaret Imrie *Hull the Lit & Phil and the world* Hull 2016.pp.264-5.

106 Ian Sumner *Despise it not* Highgate,2002.

107 Treasure House, Beverley, DDX/1282/33/2.

108 James E. Elwell(1836-1926) , a notable craftsman in wood ,active town councillor, sometime Mayor of Beverley and father of Fred Elwell R.A. Lockwood Huntley, Borough Librarian, was secretary for the fund-raising campaign.

109 Ibid.

110 Ibid. One pound and ten shilling notes were introduced in 1914 to reduce the demand for gold coins and maintain the nation's bullion deposits.

111	Treasure House, Beverley DDX1694/1/34.Three prints; one showing a crater behind a house (Eastgate House?) with onlookers, a second a close-up of the same house and a third of a crater in a field, also with onlookers.

112	A number of views of the ruins of Edwin Davis' store adjacent to Holy Trinity church were taken by Marcus Barnard , the well known marine photographer, and sold as post cards. A collection of his original glass negatives of local shipping is in the Hull Maritime Museum.

113	 This set is in the National Archives at Kew. Some of his photographs appeared in local newspapers after the end of the war. For a selection of these photographs, and notes on Charles Turner, see Credland ,2014.

114	History Centre, Hull ,TSH/2/5.

115	Also in the Hull Maritime Museum. See Credland 2014.

116	Reproduced in the editorial section of *EastYorkshire Historian*,vol.17, 2016. There is a copy in Hull Museums, acc. no. 1986.578; measures 5 by 6 ¼ in.

117	A form popular in the twentieth century for seaside and other picturesque views.

118	Best known for the numerous postcard photographs of Hull shipping thatseem to have been his chief source of income.

119	Images are: Roof of St. Thomas' church, Campbell street(Watson);House in Campbell street; Bright street, Holderness road; High street ,Hull's oldest property; Clarence street(notice Queen Victoria's portrait) [on exposed inside wall of damaged house];Church street, Drypool; House in Campbell street, Anlaby road(Watson)[sic];Campbell street, Anlaby road[sic]; Queen street(Barnard); Holy Trinity church(Barnard); Terrace in Waller street, Holderness road.

120	 By Sabine Baring-Gould (1834-1924).

121	Nicholas J. Saunders *Trench Art* Barnsley, 2011,p.90.

122	Treasure House, Beverley PE113/18.

123	Ie. no communion.

124	He died aboard HMS *Hampshire* when it struck a mine off Orkney.

125	Hull and Barnsley railway.

126	The dressing station.

127	The clock or church bell should have been silenced!

128	To quench flames in case of a fire.

129	At number 7 Anlaby road.

130	Adjutant R.C. Follett, MBE , a member of the Hull Emergency Committee, Sub-Commander, West District(Traffic). For a full list of the principal 'specials', covering all the districts of the city, see, *Hull and East Yorkshire Times* 1 February,col.5,p.3.

131	Alice Walker died when the blast carried her and the mattress on which she had been sleeping onto the roof of the church, and she fell into the pathway adjoining.

132	Angela Raby *Thomas Holme: first telephone manager, Kingston upon Hull,1903-45* (publication pending).

1a. The Blundell and Spence steam hooter, known as 'Lizzie'.

1b. Steam hooter, 'Lizzie'.

16b. Armed trawler Olivine alongside the L15.

18. Political cartoon by Ern Shaw.

19a. 50 Kilo bomb from Hull Zeppelin raids

20b, c. Brassard and pin-on badge of Special constable, J Wilson

22a, b. Brass and enamel lapel badges; front and back.